Green Road to Land's End

Cover: "These secret paths have a special magic"
Below Walker's Hill in Wiltshire

Journey's End

GREEN ROAD TO LAND'S END

Diary of a journey on foot
from London to Land's End

Roger Jones

Illustrated by Edward Dowden

EX LIBRIS PRESS

First published 1986

Ex Libris Press
1 The Shambles
Bradford on Avon
Wiltshire

Cover by 46 Design
Cover printed by R.A.Blackwell, Bradford on Avon
Typeset in 10 on 12 point Plantin
by Saxon Printing Ltd., Derby

Printed in Great Britain by
A. Wheaton & Co. Ltd, Exeter

ISBN 0 948578 01 7

To my Mother

Other books by Roger Jones:
A Book of Newton Abbot
Rambles around Newton Abbot
Where Wiltshire meets Somerset
Wiltshire Rambles
Down the Bristol Avon

Edited and introduced by Roger Jones:
The Walker's Companion
West Country Tour

CONTENTS

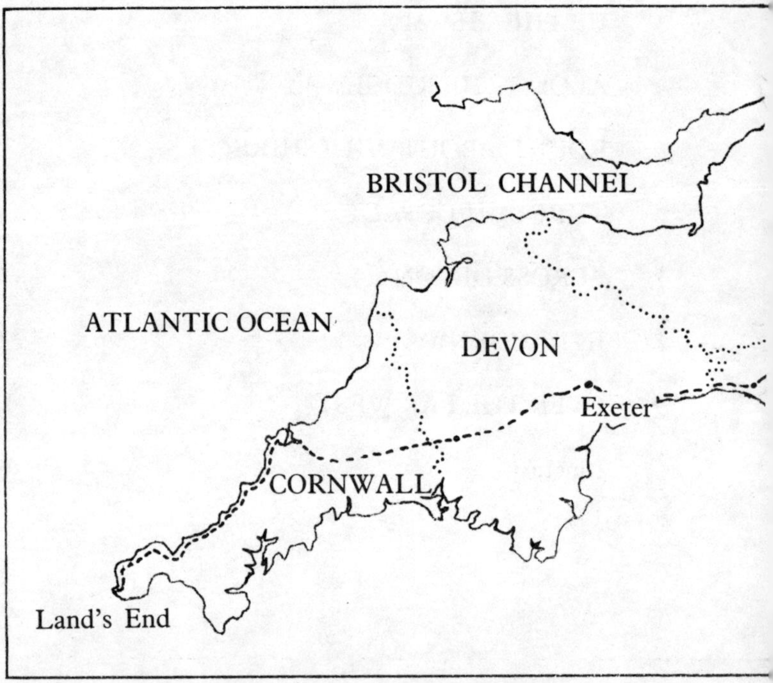

The author's route from London to Land's End

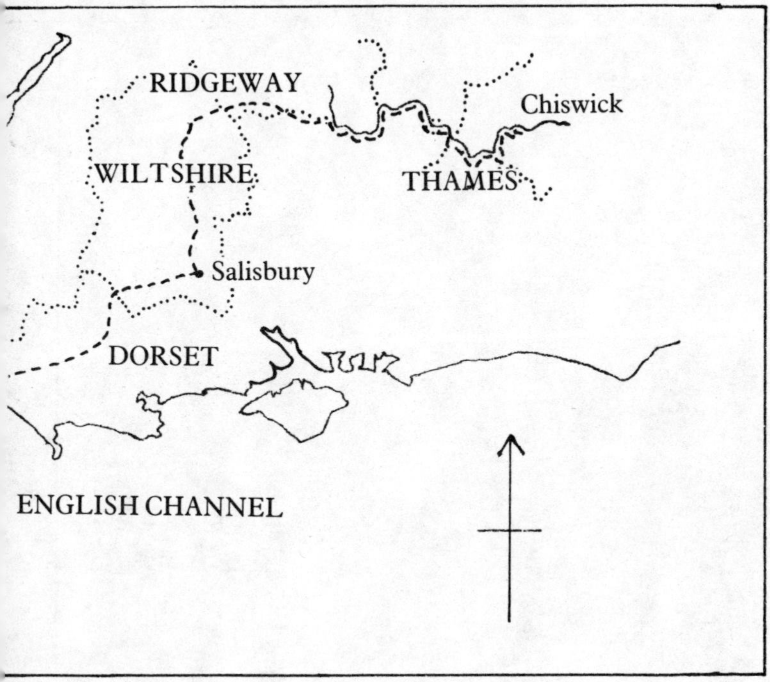
RIDGEWAY
Chiswick
WILTSHIRE
THAMES
Salisbury
DORSET
ENGLISH CHANNEL

1 INTRODUCTION

My first and very vivid memory of the English countryside was formed during a week-long camping trip which I made with my local cub pack when I was about nine years old. We pitched our tents on a slope overlooking Henley-on-Thames. It was a glorious sunny week. Cows roamed in our field and the two chief hazards were cowpats and what seemed to be a plague of wasps. There was a wood behind us which crowned the hill and sloped down the far side.

During a free afternoon a few of us ventured into the wood; one unfortunate boy stood on a wasps' nest. We were pursued down through the wood and into a field at the bottom, only to find this open space occupied by a bull. He charged at us and we scrambled over a barbed wire fence and plodded our way back to camp. There we arrived bedraggled, exhausted, our clothes torn and all of us badly stung – a bunch of city kids suddenly disillusioned with the delights of the countryside. The boy who had stood on the wasps' nest had suffered so many stings that he was taken to hospital – I myself had six which was an average number.

Notwithstanding that earlier, unfortunate episode, I'd had the idea of walking from London to Land's End for many years. For residents of West London the natural way of leaving the metropolis is to head not east, north or south, but west - up the Thames or down the A30 and into the West Country. This holds true for day trips, for holidays and also for permanent settlement. I was born in Hammersmith and spent my first 20 years in Chiswick which, like neighbouring Hammersmith, lies on the River Thames. Thus it was that I knew England to the west of London a little, but haphazardly, and very patchily.

My parents did not have a car and there were no trips out on Sundays or in the holidays, only the annual pilgrimage to my mother's home of Jersey in the Channel Islands. This meant two weeks or more playing on the beach or in the sea – but only once a walk in the country, an occasion I remember with fondness. As a teenager I began to go further afield with my friends - one of our favourite escapades was to catch the train from Richmond to one of the Thameside watering places such as Runnymede, or Windsor, or Henley and there to hire a couple of boats and spend the day messing about in them. There would be races, landings on islands, splashings, duckings and usually some illicit cider drinking which only added to the merriment.

When I left school and went to college I joined a small group of students on a week-long geological expedition to Dorset. We camped at Corfe and surveyed much of the coast between Studland and Weymouth in the course of the week. In the mid-1960s I intended to take up mining engineering at the Camborne School of Mines in Cornwall. As a preliminary to the three year course I was introduced to work underground during two weeks at the mine just outside Camborne where Holman's, the mining equipment company, test their products. This was followed by a longer spell at the Geevor tin mine near St Just where I gained experience in all manner of mining tasks.

I got married in 1970 and my family and I left Chiswick in 1974 to live on a small estate of modern houses in Wokingham, near Reading, in Berkshire. Most of the other young families there had similarly moved from West London to the nearest moderately priced housing giving reasonable access to Heathrow and London. In 1976 we moved to Newton Abbot in South Devon which was even more of a change than Berkshire. The pace and way of life seemed to me slower and more amenable in Wokingham as compared with Chiswick but Newton Abbot was slower again. Wokingham is a town of character but it is somewhat overshadowed by London and much of its population commutes there to work each day.

Newton Abbot, by contrast, is a provincial town whose development over the centuries and very existence seems to speak for itself when viewed from one of the hills which overlooks it. It lies at the head of an estuary, at the confluence of a number of valleys and at the junction of road and rail routes. The weekly market provides the necessary focus for a large catchment area of farms and villages roundabout as it has done since medieval times.

It was in Newton Abbot that history, i.e. the story of people in a landscape, first began to mean something to me. It was when I was living there, too, that I began to explore the countryside, though still fearful of any creature on four legs larger than a field mouse. I walked much of the magnificent South Devon coast path but favoured local walks by the quiet and unspoilt Teign estuary, and by the overgrown footpaths, bridleways and deep sunken lanes which led past abandoned mills and old barns to hidden farms and ancient villages.

Dartmoor did not especially attract me – I preferred to drive across it than to walk over it. Perhaps I was still too much of a city-bred pedestrian who preferred the constant reminders of humanity in the inter-urban landscape of Newton Abbot and Torbay to the wild, bleak and windswept uplands of Dartmoor.

In 1980 we moved back east to the old cloth town of Bradford on Avon – a few miles from Bath – in the county of Wiltshire. The countryside here is similar to that about Newton Abbot in that it is laid thickly with small towns, villages and farms with many reminders of former industrial activity. I wrote a book of walks in this area as I had done on the country in South Devon. On the strength of these a publisher asked me to do one for the whole county of Wiltshire and this took me, among other places, to the wide chalk downs of Wiltshire which, in their open aspect at least, bear some resemblance to Dartmoor. A later pursuit was to follow our local River Avon from its source in the north-western corner of the county along its 75 miles to the sea. Rivers have a special fascination and it had been an unfulfilled wish to follow one from end to end.

For even longer I had promised myself that sometime I would walk from London to Land's End; by doing so I should be able to link together all those known and recognisable bits of the West Country. It would be interesting to see not just the chalk downs, Dartmoor and the granite cliffs of Cornwall, but to observe one land with many aspects and all gradually evolving, at walking pace, from one into another.

Having decided to undertake this journey I had to work out a route from London to Land's End. The most direct road link is the A30 which actually begins in Chiswick and heads directly south-west to reach Penzance some 300 miles later, and many is the time I have hitch-hiked it, ridden it on a motor scooter and driven it, but it could not be considered as a walking route. Much as I like to avoid the beaten track I felt it would make sense to use recognised long-distance footpaths where convenient. The alternative was to plot a course cross-country using footpaths wherever possible. The difficulty here is that there is no knowing whether a path which is marked quite clearly on the Ordnance Survey map is at all clear or even passable on the ground. Whilst country lanes and minor roads are quite acceptable for walking, A-roads and the like most certainly are not.

I planned to leave London at Chiswick, my first home, by walking to the Thames and following it upstream as far as Goring where I would leave the river to follow the Ridgeway Long Distance Footpath to Avebury and from thence to Pewsey in the heart of Wiltshire. From there I would follow the Old Marlborough Road across a section of Salisbury Plain bounded to the north by Pewsey Vale and to the west by the Salisbury Avon. This would take me to Amesbury and from there I would find my way south by lane and footpath via Old Sarum to Salisbury.

From Salisbury I would take another old coach road towards Shaftesbury which follows the ridge between the valleys of the

Nadder and Ebble. At White Sheet Hill, overlooking the A30, I would head south and south west across Cranborne Chase, along the North Dorset Downs to Cerne Abbas, then south-west to link up with the Dorset Coast Path and into Devon. At some point in East Devon I should forsake the coast path and head cross-country towards Exeter. From Exeter due west towards the River Teign to follow that river upstream to Chagford, then across Dartmoor to Tavistock; from here I would head due west by country lane and footpath across East Cornwall to Padstow on the coast. From here I would follow the North Cornwall Coast Path, though not religiously, to Land's End.

My first plan was to complete the walk in five stages, over five weeks and coming home at weekends. As the time for my departure approached I began to realise that this was not a good idea – I should lose the sense of a long, continuous walk, and it would take longer overall, to say nothing of the additional expense incurred in travelling to and fro. The first section would be the easiest – the flat, well-trodden Thames towpath would act as a warm up for the second stage: the Ridgeway through Berkshire and Wiltshire which I thought would be fairly straightforward and undemanding. The most difficult part I guessed would be the North Cornwall Coast Path towards the end of the walk. This route I reckoned to be upwards of 400 miles – I would have to cover a good 20 miles per day to reach my destination in the three weeks I finally had alotted myself from May Day Bank Holiday to Spring Bank Holiday.

Another question to be decided was where to stay each night. I did not want my walk organised to the extent that I would book my lodgings for the night in advance. Did I want lodgings? Should I not take a sleeping bag or a blanket and make a bed in some convenient haybarn? My wife pooh-poohed the idea and I must say I was rather glad she did. Instead of a warm haystack, in which I have always dreamed of sleeping, I should probably end up on a hard bench in some graffiti-emblazoned bus shelter beside an A-road. I would seek out bed and breakfast accommodation each evening but take a sleeping bag in case I got stuck or in case I felt disposed to fulfil that ambition of spending a night in a haystack.

I am not an equipment minded person and, in addition to maps, I planned to take the minimum necessary for my comfort. Thus it was that I set out from Chiswick on the morning of May Day Bank Holiday, 1984.

2 AWAY FROM HOME

Monday 7th May

A cool breeze and a blue sky studded with occasional fair weather cumulus clouds greeted me as I set out from my mother's home in West London to walk to Land's End. Months, in fact years, of anticipation lent a feeling of elation as I walked along the familiar streets of childhood towards the River Thames.

My parents had moved into part of a large Victorian house on the edge of Bedford Park in Chiswick in 1945, the year I was born. Bedford Park was built during the 1870s and 80s and became known as the first garden suburb; Norman Shaw was the architect responsible for much of the estate. The houses exhibit a dazzling mixture of styles. Here are bay windows, Dutch gables, dormers set in steeply pitched roofs, balconies, and much which is drawn from traditional English vernacular architecture. Red brick and red tiles are used in contrast to the usual yellow London stock and grey slates. Not surprisingly, Bedford Park attracted as residents many figures from the worlds of art and literature and even produced a weekly newspaper for a period. The whole estate is built in a rough arc which fans out from the remarkable Church of St Michael's, the Tabard Inn and the former village stores. Nearby too is Turnham Green Station which was opened in 1869 by the London and South Western Railway. The station faces Acton Green, a wedge of open space bounded by the railway embankment and a line of mature and stately horse chestnuts.

I turned westwards along the Bath Road, believed to lie on the course of the Roman road leading from the capital via Brentford to the west, past those homely sounding streets: Rupert Road, Priory Gardens, Woodstock Road, then left past the station and under the railway bridge upon which the electric trains rumble and under which roosts a flock of London pigeons. Turnham Green Terrace and its shops led me across Chiswick High Road and into Devonshire Road and another face of Chiswick, though the contrast is now certainly not as marked as I remember as a child.

I have an old map of London dated *c.*1890 which shows Chiswick still isolated from Hammersmith and Acton by a green belt of open fields. Bedford Park is built up and Devonshire Road is unaltered, although its northern end is given as Chiswick Field Lane. Presumably the latter became a misnomer when Chiswick Field surrendered to bricks and mortar. The streets around Devonshire Road are given the appellation "Chiswick New Town" and this district of cheap, basic, terraced houses must have constituted a kind of model estate for the working classes, many of whom were no doubt employed as domestic staff by the middle class folk north of Chiswick High Road. I became familiar with Bedford Park through doing an early morning paper round and got to know the streets of Chiswick New Town by helping my father with his milk round on Saturdays and in the school holidays.

Until 1945 my father and mother had lived with my father's family over the family shop in Fraser Street, a turning off Devonshire Road. My father's three sisters organised the shop, whilst the three brothers ran the dairy, situated in the back yard. All was presided over by grandfather, a stout and tyrannical looking old man with a Kaiser moustache who died during the war and whom I only know from photographs.

In Bedford Park the houses are arranged along Avenues, Groves and Gardens, but here they are Streets or, at best, Roads. The names too, are generally less evocative of Old England, except perhaps for Dale Street and Glebe Street (this district was built on Church land). More typical is Binns Road, Reckitt Road and Quick Street. Glebe Street led me to Dale Street, then to Fraser Street. The houses of the former Chiswick New Town still exist as far south as Fraser Street. The area has been renamed by the estate agents as the Glebe Estate or "Chiswick's Little Chelsea". Artisans' terraced houses are advertised as "charming cottage" or "bijou residence". The entire area is fast becoming gentrified: young professionals move in as houses become vacant and change hands for sums that have even outstripped inflation over the past 15 years or so – up to £60,000 at the time of walking.

Long gone too are my family's shop and dairy. These were situated on the side of Fraser Street which was pulled down in a slum clearance programme in the early sixties. The southern chunk of Chiswick New Town was demolished and replaced by brick-built council flats with pitched roofs which rise from two to six storeys and actually help retain some of the traditional atmosphere of the area, by housing many of the former residents. Gone are the corner off-licence and local master baker but the fish and chip shop is still there and so is the Chiswick Mission.

People were flocking into the latter as I passed by the house in Fraser Street where we had our first flat after getting married in 1970. Devonshire Street leads into Bennett Street, although streets seem to lose their meaning when not flanked by rows of houses but only by occasional blocks of flats. The White Swan, known locally as the Mucky Duck, has gone and is almost unrecognisable as a suite of offices. I had by now reached the London Extension of the M4 which loses motorway status at Chiswick Flyover but continues as a six lane dual carriageway - this is the road which carries all the traffic to Heathrow Airport. I walked towards Hogarth Roundabout where the extended M4 meets the extended M3 and which was said, surely not without truth, to be the busiest road junction in the country.

Across the road, behind a high brick wall, lie the grounds of Chiswick House, the house itself a splendid Palladian villa erected by Richard Boyle, Earl of Burlington, around 1730, though not visible from here. Next door is the former Hogarth Laundry where I worked in the summer holidays of 1961 – the year I failed my O-levels. Perhaps it was that experience which persuaded me to resit those exams. The old laundry is now occupied by a point of sale display company. Nestling behind a brick wall between the former laundry and former Cherry Blossom Shoe Polish factory (rebuilding in 1984 as 58,500 square feet of offices) sits Hogarth House, a delightful building dating from about 1700 in which the artist William Hogarth lived from 1749 until his death in 1765.

A television programme about Hogarth's life I once saw portrayed Hogarth and friend in that house, every period detail about the house, the friends' conversation and their costume quite correct. They strolled through the garden and opened the gate, only to be confronted by the terrible roar of that six-lane highway outside. This they greeted with a look of horror. A biographer of Hogarth wrote in 1904 of his house that "The breezy expanse of the surroundings must have braced and refreshed the painter after his sedentary work and acted as a balm to his ruffled temperament and to the failing health of his latter days." May he rest in peace.

I can just remember the days before road improvements when Chiswick High Road was choked with heavy traffic and Hogarth Lane was a narrow, winding way. Hogarth is now perhaps chiefly known to the nation for the indispensable traffic roundabout named after him. A single lane flyover traverses this (built as a temporary structure some twenty years ago) but the pedestrian must descend to a system of subways to cross the roads hereabouts. This muggers' paradise led me to the south side of the screaming highway, to Church Street and quite suddenly to yet another face of Chiswick.

The gem of Church Street is signposted "The Old Burlington Founded 15th Century", a charming timber framed house, formerly a pub. Chiswick Parish Church, St Nicholas, stands nearby. In its graveyard are buried the remains of my sister, my only sibling, who died as a baby before I was born. Straight ahead the road leads down to a gap where a slipway meets the river. It was from here that the former Chiswick Ferry once plied its trade. Upstream is a mainly industrial area, downstream is Chiswick Mall – an architectural delight. Here are some fine residences, mainly Georgian, and probably with even more literary and artistic associations than Bedford Park. One of the first houses, Walpole House, was once a preparatory school attended by W.M.Thackeray. It later became the model for Miss Pinkerton's Seminary for Young Ladies in Thackeray's *Vanity Fair*. On page 1 of that book he writes:

> While the present century was in its teens, and on one sunshiny morning in June, there drove up to the great iron gate of Miss Pinkerton's academy for young ladies, on Chiswick Mall, a large family coach, with two fat horses in blazing harness, driven by a fat coachman in a three-cornered hat and a wig, at the rate of four miles an hour.

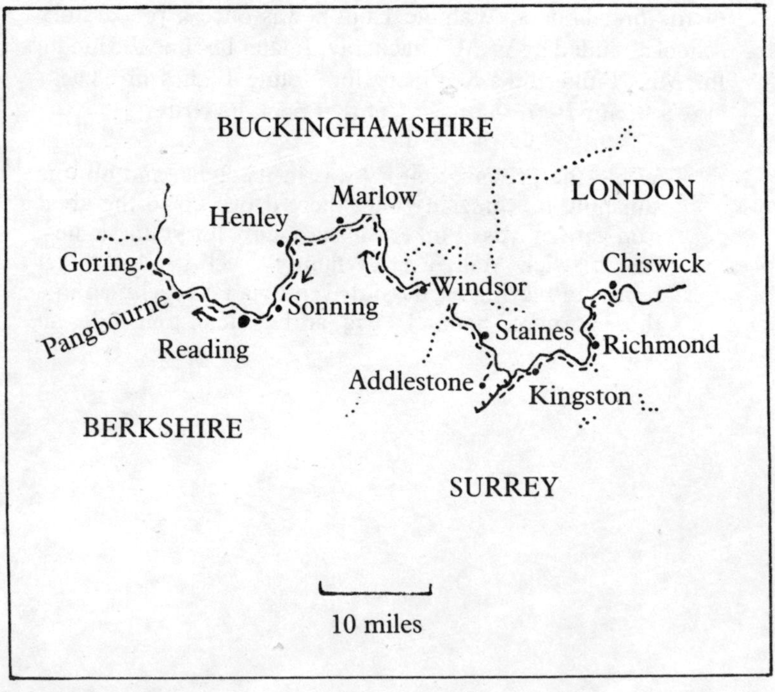

Up the Thames

3 UP THE THAMES

Now my walk was truly about to begin. The first stage of my "Green Road to Land's End" was to be the Thames towpath. There is really no exit from the capital which is as green and pleasant and far from traffic as this. I would, however, not be able to reach the towpath until I could cross the river. From the site of the former Chiswick Ferry I had to forsake the river where industrial premises monopolise the water frontage. I reached the former Chiswick Open Air Swimming Pool, now sadly no more, having given way to more luxurious indoor facilities with saunas in other parts of the borough. The Open Air Swimming Pool, now derelict, covered an enormous site. There were two pools, one very large and both with diving boards, together with a vast paved area for sunbathing and running about; the whole surrounded by hundreds of individual changing cubicles. I loved swimming as a child and always had a season ticket for the duration. The pools opened in early May when the water temperature could be in the low forties; my ideal temperature was 65°F.

A flood of memories came to me as I walked around the perimeter wall: of hours spent in that chlorinated water, of endless practice dives but only once from the top board, of losing my clothes on one occasion, of machines that dispensed a glob of Brylcreem for one old penny, of bikes and bits of bikes pinched from the cycle shed.

I turned down the avenue of lime trees beside a park with swings on my right and the Edensor Road Council Estate on my left. This estate, built immediately post-war, consists of low-rise blocks of flats and looked remarkably attractive in its maturity – plenty of grass and trees between the red brick walls and balconies. The avenue leads to the river and Chiswick Promenade, or "The Prom" as it is known locally.

Grassy terraces lead down to a wide path beside a sloping concrete bank in the fissures of which grow crack willows. The path leads to a bandstand and on past boathouses. I ascended Barnes railway bridge and crossed the river by a footpath beside the track; the river was choppy in the stiff breeze. I descended the far side and joined the Thames towpath to follow the south bank of the river as far as Kingston. I noticed the river ebbing fast as I continued past Watneys brewery at Mortlake, and the *White Hart* pub, once (and perhaps still) famous for its live jazz.

A spray can message on the wall facing the river here read "Punks and Anarchists Unite – Riot Against the Police". I wondered how many punks and anarchists were likely to see this notice from the river or the towpath. It was now mid-morning and there were numerous joggers running along the path. I walked under the elegant, modern Chiswick Bridge with its three wide arches. More graffiti here: apart from the usual "Chelsea" and "QPR" the tantalising question, "Who Created the Creator?"

On my left now stood Mortlake Crematorium, a not unattractive brick building with a sweeping drive through well tended gardens up to its main entrance. It looked vaguely churchy in a sort of Byzantine way. I had been to "The Crem" twice in recent years, once for the cremation of an old friend's father and, in 1982, of my own father. I remembered the service and the "appreciation" of my father which I'd read out, the silence we'd had, the very sympathetic parson, the coffin, there one minute and vanished through the drapes the next. And then outside: the wreaths, the red eyes and that curiously sweet smell from the chimney. It was bank holiday today and, although people were presumably dying they were not being cremated and there was no smell.

Past the crematorium I looked out for a dirt track where I

used to go on my bike as a child. Once I went with a friend and we were challenged by some tough kids as to which side of the river we came from. It was only my bad geography that saved me from a thumping. On the north bank I passed Cubitt's Yard, formerly a boat yard but now a luxury housing development. This was not as attractive as a 1930s block of flats further along which, flanking the wide river, puts one in mind of an old ocean liner, with the horizontal lines of its white-painted balconies like decks and central tower resembling a funnel. Under another railway bridge and I stood opposite Strand on the Green with its well known pubs the *Bull's Head*, the *City Barge* and the *Steam Packet*. The *Packet* was the last pub I was taken to on my stag night which I insisted on having a week before I got married, not the night before, in order not to risk missing the ceremony.

The pier at Kew Bridge bore an official notice: "Keep London Nuclear Free"; I gave the GLC a silent cheer. There used to be a fairground behind the pub on the south side of Kew Bridge: a pit full of noise, garish colours, dubious characters and great excitement. I found that this had been replaced by tennis courts. There seems to be an inexorable move up-market: open-air swimming pools into saunas, boatyards into luxury homes, fairgrounds into tennis courts.

The towpath now follows the perimeter of Kew Gardens; on the far bank stands Brentford. Brentford certainly used to be down-market with its gas works, docks, football ground, street corner pubs and fish and chip shops. Had Brentford changed too? I knew it had, of course. Long gone are the gasworks, though the holders still stand as a reminder. The trolley buses used to glide through Brentford and between the high walls of the gasworks. Here smoke and gas and grit discharged from various orifices and the air grew dark and stinking. Brentford High street has been undergoing "redevelopment" and has suffered planning blight for as long as I can remember.

Brentford now is dominated by half a dozen very high tower blocks which seem uncomfortably close to the main flight path into Heathrow Airport. The tower of the old waterworks has been preserved – it was said because it was too expensive to demolish – and the site now houses a Steam Museum. Two islands, or eyots, stand in the river beyond Kew Bridge and between them one can see St George's Church, now redundant but which for many years has housed a remarkable collection of organs and pianolas and is known as "The Piano Museum".

Prior to the keyboards it housed a large number of books which formed the Layton Collection. Thomas Layton was an eccentric and maniacal collector of almost anything, particularly books, and lived in the toll house at Kew Bridge. He would pay the itinerant bargees and boatmen handsomely for any book or antiquity they turned up. I had the task, in 1970, of sorting through this miscellany of some 20,000 volumes and putting them into a semblance of order. They had been moved from the pews and aisles of St George's Church to the muniments room at the rear of Chiswick Town Hall. In the church the books had been gnawed by rats and defecated upon by pigeons so some were in a very poor state. The Layton Collection, though for many years forgotten, has become a *cause célèbre* in the Borough of Hounslow with various groups fighting for its preservation.

Past Brentford eyots I reached the confluence of the Grand Union Canal, once a thriving dock and now signposted as "Entrance to Pleasure Cruising Waterways" and "Brentford Marina and Yacht Club". Charles G. Harper, writing in his book *Rural Nooks around London*, published *c.*1910, writes of the bustling commercial life of Brentford and of its "busy and crowded docks." The former railway goods yard has now been redeveloped, inevitably it seems, as a sprawl of "luxury homes".

On my left the scene was beautified by the rhododendrons and bluebells of Kew Gardens. On the opposite bank the eye was drawn towards the stately pile of Syon House, its flat roof surmounted by a huge golden lion. The landscaping here was done by Capability Brown at the time when the house was built on the site of a 15th century nunnery occupied by the "Daughters of Sion". Now all was green and open to the sky, though the prospect was intermittently submerged by the ear-shattering scream of jet-engined aircraft homing in on Heathrow. Yet birds were here too: mallards, swans, Canada geese and black headed gulls.

After Syon Park comes Isleworth: another former "Rural Nook around London" with its church and riverside pub the *London Apprentice* where my wedding reception was held fourteen years previously. The Royal Botanic Gardens of Kew merge into Old Deer Park which floods regularly when the river is high. Richmond Lock is the first lock on the Thames though only used at low water. Richmond brought back more memories: of walks along the river with girlfriends, of visits to riverside pubs and clubs.

The towpath continues below Richmond Hill, past Petersham Church where I had once attended someone's wedding ceremony and on to Eel Pie Island at Twickenham. Yet more poignant memories here: of Sunday nights spent at the Jazz Club – of bands like Long John Baldry and the Hoochie Coochie Men, Georgie Fame and the Blue Flames, The Ground Hogs, the Yardbirds, Rod Stewart. That dilapidated old building with its springy dance floor, filthy lavatories, ubiquitous graffiti, weird looking people and enormous range of keg beers seemed the perfect answer to our youthful rejection of parental ideas of a nice place to go in the evenings. I loved it - Sunday night at the Island was the high point of the week. All that has since been swept away and tacky houses built over the site.

I'd walked about ten miles and my feet were feeling hot and sore. The previous evening I had walked the three miles from Kensington Bus Station to Chiswick and had the beginnings of a blister. Now I had a cup of tea and a bar of chocolate and rested for no longer than ten minutes. To stop any longer, I thought, would be unwise.

The far side of the river from Teddington to Kingston was

taken up by private houses with long lovely gardens sweeping down to private moorings on the river. At Kingston Bridge I changed banks to follow the towpath, now with fewer people, beside Hampton Court Park to reach Hampton Court Palace itself. There were more boats now, in fact an endless procession of pleasure boats chugging up and down.

I stared through the railings at the amazingly complex facade, roofs and chimneys of the Palace before crossing the bridge and the stalls selling tourist junk and the like to reclaim the towpath once more. Molesey Lock showed the record floodmarks of 1821 and 1894. By now my pace was slowing – my legs were tired and my feet felt quite sore. But it was best not to dwell on this discomfort. I plodded on past house boats - many of them not really boats but rather small bungalows on floating platforms. Passing by the reservoirs at Molesey reminded me of one of the wilder schemes of the late 1960s – to lace London's water supply with a liberal dose of the mind-expanding drug LSD. It was thought that if the population of our capital, including the government, was "turned on", the Golden Age would dawn at last.

A bank holiday fair was in full swing beside the river at Walton where I bought a cup of tea and a sandwich. A little further on, I sat down beside the entrance to Desborough Cut (named after Lord Desborough, a former chairman of the Thames Conservancy). This cut is a direct waterway between Walton and Weybridge which avoids a lengthy meander via Sunbury. The state of my feet persuaded me to take this shorter route. I took off my shoes and socks and plunged my feet into the cold river hoping that, by some magic, such drastic action would alleviate the soreness. Keeping a watchful eye for marauding pike I sat bathing my lower extremities, notwithstanding the gaze of the occupants of a passing police launch. When I redressed, my feet felt just as bad, if not worse, and I hobbled my way upriver. Keep looking around, lose myself in the surroundings, I told myself, which is what I usually do quite naturally.

At Weybridge I continued according to plan; that is, I crossed the Wey Navigation and bore left along its towpath. My first night I'd arranged to stay with some friends at Addlestone which I knew was near the Wey. I followed the towpath to a former flour mill, and here left the waterway to follow field paths towards a road. Just as I left the last gate to reach the pavement my right foot exploded. That is, something gave way which produced a sudden stab of pain. I guessed it was a blister bursting. I shuffled along the road, past a chiropodist's surgery (!) and found my friend's house. Everybody was out so I sat in the back garden until it grew too cold to bear. They were still out. In any other circumstances I would have gone for a walk to pass the time .... in any other circumstances. I hobbled out to the front of the house and found the pub up the road open. A pint of beer in front of a roaring log fire and a conversation to eavesdrop was a taste of heaven after an hour sitting in a cold garden with sore feet. I had a second pint and hung it out until I felt sure that the journey back to my friends' house would find them at home.

Indeed they were. It was good to see them and to sit down to some hot food. I went around barefoot for the rest of the evening hoping that this would cure my foot problems.

Tuesday 8th May

The next morning I left my friends and their children and set out to regain the Thames at Chertsey Bridge; I purchased a bottle of surgical spirit, which had been recommended for my feet, at a chemist's on the way. Crossing Chertsey Bridge I joined the towpath on the north bank, passing under the M3 beside wide meadows studded with willows. The only activity here on the day after Bank Holiday was a bloke collecting rubbish and a few swans gliding imperiously about the river.

Beyond the meadows the houses begin - this is Laleham Terrace – such fine houses and such remarkably well kept gardens. It looks like any well-to-do suburban street except that here the houses face a river instead of a tarmacadamed road. It was a fine sunny day though cool – perfect walking weather, in fact - if only my feet had been in better condition. On my first day I reckoned I'd walked around 24 miles and that was the sort of average I would have to keep up if I was to reach Land's End in my allotted three weeks. I thought I was used to walking long distances. The truth was that on the occasional days when I walked in Wiltshire or Somerset I rarely exceeded ten or twelve miles and that was usually pretty leisurely – visiting village churches or perhaps stopping for a pub lunch. I've never possessed a pair of walking boots: I made something of a virtue of not going in for a lot of special equipment to pursue an activity which is, after all, as basic to man's natural condition as eating or sleeping. I had bought what I thought was a pair of sensible walking shoes and tried them out on a day's hike on the Marlborough Downs. My feet had been a little sore at the end of the day but I was sure would not be so the next time.

Having walked twenty four miles in these shoes in one day my feet were abominably sore and blistered. I sat down at Chertsey Bridge and applied the surgical spirit which felt good as I was dabbing it on but as soon as I'd squeezed my swelling feet back into those so-called sensible shoes and taken a few steps I felt my lower extremities as tender as before. But on I plodded, past those *Homes and Gardens* homes and gardens, along the towpath from which nothing is now towed and beside the river which adds so much value to the properties on its banks. I sang as I plodded, "Give me strength in my feet, keep me walking", to the evangelical tune "Give me joy in my heart, keep me praising". At Staines I crossed the bridge to reach the towpath which now runs along the south side of the river. Under the A30 and on to Runnymede – a wide open space beneath the eminence of Coopers Hill, the latter crowned with the Commonwealth Air Forces Memorial. I had visited this once many years before – there had been many middle-aged couples laying flowers beneath the names of incredibly young men who had died in action – it was a moving experience.

Runnymede means "The Meadow in Council Island" and was evidently an ancient meeting place. It was here or on the nearby island that King John and the barons signed Magna Carta in 1215. As I said, it was the custom among my friends to visit riverside watering places, such as Runnymede, on Bank Holidays. Before any of us had a car we would catch the train. One evening, or possibly early one morning, a vanload of us had pulled up at Runnymede and, a little more daring for a few drinks, had stripped off and had a moonlit swim.

All I could think about on Day 2 of my walk was the state of my feet: I sat down to dab on another application of surgical spirit. In the course of attending to other bodily needs my toilet roll fell into the river. As I watched it sail away it seemed to symbolise the irrevocable loss of all the comforts one expects of life in the late twentieth century .... irrevocable for the next three weeks, anyway.

Further along the towpath I entered the Royal County of Berkshire and passed by the *Bells Of Ouseley* – a pub I'd once frequented. Here was a notice board which proclaimed "Road to Egham and Staines except at high water". There was no chance of flooding now – spring had been exceptionally dry this year. Beyond Ham Island I crossed Albert Bridge to follow the road to Datchet; this is necessary because the open space between here and Windsor is part of Windsor Great Park which is closed to the public.

After the village centre it is possible to avoid the road by following a right of way along the edge of a golf course. Unfortunately I missed the way out of here to the road, Victoria Bridge and the riverside route. Instead I continued along the right of way until I reached Black Potts Railway Bridge. Here I realised my mistake but, given the state of my feet, was not prepared to go back the way I'd come. Instead, I clambered up the embankment, listened for the sound of approaching trains and, when all was silent, shuffled across as speedily as I could. I was descending the far side when a train crossed. Here I had to climb over a railing – I tossed my rucksack over first and jumped from the top of the railings onto my poor feet. I sat down, discarded my shoes and socks and, listening to the distant roar of traffic on the M4, let my feet take the air.

I dragged myself on to Romney Lock with its view across to Eton College Chapel. At Windsor Bridge, having walked about 14 miles, I felt I'd reached a low point. It was another 10 or 11 miles to Bourne End via Maidenhead. From Bourne End I intended to summon some friends who lived at Wycombe Marsh not far away, where I planned to spend the night. At Windsor I thought I might catch a boat up-river to Maidenhead: unfortunately no boats were running. I had a cup of tea and a sandwich and just knew I couldn't walk any further. I stumbled along to the station and caught any number of trains until I eventually reached Bourne End. Feeling more of a coward and a cheat by the minute I waited for a bus. Every time I catch a bus, which is about once every five years, I am astonished at the fares charged. A pound is never enough – it always seems to be a case of changing a fiver to ride a few miles. I hadn't visited my friends for several years and bought a bottle of wine at a corner shop on the way. I was welcomed, given a cup of coffee and recommended witch hazel for my feet. It smelt nicer than surgical spirit and reminded me of my wife (her name's Hazel) and really did seem to have a soothing effect. By now I blamed my rotten sensible shoes for the appalling state of my feet. My host's son had recommended his "Fell Boots" which were to be had at £5 a pair in nearby High Wycombe.

Wednesday 9th May

Next morning my friend drove me into town and we waited for the shop to open. I bought a pair of Fell Boots. They have suede uppers on flexible rubber soles and are lined with a soft fleecy material. They felt a great relief. I was driven on to Marlow by my kind host and deposited by the bridge. I very much regretted having to miss the towpath from Windsor to Marlow and promised myself I'd walk that section sometime.

The suspension bridge at Marlow was built in the 1830s and is quite striking. Day 3 was another perfect day – clear, sunny but cool. I felt my heart lift as I crossed the river – I was still concious of my feet but they felt much less uncomfortable in my Spanish Fell Boots.

The route passed cottages and the church at Bisham, by Bisham Abbey and turned into a charming, shady track which eventually became a path through open fields. Rather than heading off to reach the towpath via Hurley Lock I continued along field paths and tracks until I reached the riverside again before Medmenham. At Medmenham the Thames Walk follows the right of way below Culham Court, with its sloping lawns and steps reaching down to the river.

The lane at Aston bears down to the river and the *Flower Pot Hotel*, a somewhat remote riverside inn with an old noticeboard which reads, "Food and Accommodation for Fishing and Boating Parties". The towpath again and a splendid view of Hambledon Mill which I'd never seen before: it is a large and magnificent white-painted weatherboarded mill which was still functioning as such in 1958. According to the Ramblers Association guide to the Thames Walk: "A spectacular right of way crosses the lock and a succession of weirs to pass by the mill and reach the north bank." This was a temptation to loiter and explore and one which I would not normally resist. I had many miles to walk and did not want to squander my limited physical resources.

Hambledon Mill: "a large and magnificent white-painted, weatherboarded mill"

The gently curving towpath eventually reached Temple Island and the wide straight stretch of the Thames above Henley, known as Henley Reach. The midday sunshine had awakened the butterflies - peacocks and brimstones fluttered about the path. This is where the Henley Regatta is held every first week of July, an annual fixture begun in 1839. There were two months to go before the event but work was already underway on the special piling along the riverside which marks the course, artificially straightened in the early 1920s. Marquees were being erected and Hobbs and Son, the Henley boat business founded in 1870, were busy, as they are every year from Easter until August, constructing and dismantling for the Regatta.

Henley on Thames is a most attractive riverside town. In the period during the 1970s when I had lived near Reading, the rural peace and watering places of Oxfordshire regularly attracted my family and me north of the river. I became interested in traditional brewing (through imbibing quantities of its product), of which there is much in this part of the Thames Valley, and spent a morning at Brakspear's Brewery in Henley. I was employed as a branch librarian at the time and justified this pursuit as essential research for a local history display entitled "Breweries of the Thames Valley". I also visited the old Courage Brewery (née Simonds) in Reading and Morland's in Abingdon.

I had promised myself when I set out on my walk that I would not indulge in any pub lunches, nor even a lunchtime pint. To do so would inevitably slow my progress and blunt my response to my surroundings. In practice I found that I was rarely tempted. I discovered that it was unwise to stop for more than about 15 minutes. The longer one rested the harder it was to resume walking. One lost the rhythm and one's feet seem to swell when not in use. I sat briefly outside a riverside snack bar imbibing a can of Seven Up and chewing a Mars Bar. The pubs I ignored, and the church and the almshouses and the bright, lively High Street and the second-hand bookshops.

I was soon on my feet again and trekking along the footpath past the playground and fields where I had often been with my children, past an island that was up for sale and on to Marsh Lock. The towpath now crosses the water over a long wooden causeway to Marsh Island and back to the mainland again. Soon I had to leave the towpath and follow minor roads; I waited for a train to pass before crossing the line above Shiplake Railway Station. I regained the river at Shiplake Lock where a heron alighted and gracefully flew away.

The towpath between Shiplake and Sonning is a charming unspoilt stretch. Flat meadows stretch away on the south bank marked only by willows and clumps of grazing Frisian cattle. The footpath passes an occasional boggy patch where comfrey and marsh marigold grow. Swans inhabit the river and, on this day, intermittent rowing boats passed full of young gentlemen

"I waited for a train to pass before crossing the line above Shiplake Railway Station"

from nearby Shiplake College. They were exhorted to pull harder by somebody with a megaphone in a small boat with an outboard motor. It all seemed a bit pointless in this otherwise calm and peaceful setting.

The sun was high and bright and when I reached a sandy shore I dropped my rucksack, took off my footwear and paddled. The miracle cure I'd hoped for did not take place .... I put my shoes and socks back on and limped away. The eight and a half miles from Marlow to Henley had really not been too bad on my feet but by now the excruciating soreness was developing once again, fell boots notwithstanding. As I approached Sonning Bridge the sun ducked behind a bank of cloud and the day changed character in an instant. Now it was grey and dull and felt much colder. I changed banks at Sonning.

Here I was very close to Woodley, the community where I had worked for two years as branch librarian. Woodley is almost entirely made up of rather basic owner-occupied houses built since the war, many of which have been constructed on the former Reading Aerodrome. Almost everyone commutes: to Reading, Slough, Heathrow, London. Woodley is virtually a new town, with a population ten years ago of 30,000 plus but without the infrastructure and facilities which one expects to find in such a community, though hopefully things have improved since I was there. The library was entirely inadequate for the size of the population. The development around Reading continues unabated; regulations maintaining the Green Belt have been disregarded and the ensuing sprawl nicknamed "Heseltown" after the then M.P. for Henley, Michael Heseltine (later Environment supremo).

Like Henley, Sonning appears safe - a Thameside gem protected from unwanted development. I changed banks at Sonning Bridge to follow the south bank to Reading. This section did not seem so memorable but that may be owing to the changed weather conditions. There are gravel pits on the opposite bank where it seemed odd to see a sheet of water at a level lower than the river. The distant view of the gas holders and office blocks of Reading grew closer by the minute as I approached Sonning. Reaching the River Kennet, where craft can gain access to the Kennet and Avon Canal which links the Thames with the Bristol Avon, I turned left, under the mainline railway bridge and along the towpath flanked by old pubs and a brand new and not unattractive high density housing development known as Orts Road.

Some steps led me up to a road bridge and I emerged at the Huntley and Palmers Biscuit Factory. I'd arranged to stay with some friends not seen since my Woodley days and here I bore left in the direction of Earley where they lived. I tried a Chinese Restaurant but it was only takeaway. Eventually I settled on a Kebab House near the junction with London Road. It was also takeaway and pretty ghastly, but I'd told my friends I should not want a meal – it was cheek enough to be asking for the use of a bed after ten years.

My host showed me some splendid photographs of a walk he had done the previous year. It was A.Wainwright's Coast to Coast Walk from Robin Hood's Bay to St Bees Head – it covers some of England's best and wildest hill country including the North York Moors, the Pennines and the Lake District Mountains. He had walked over 200 miles in 10 days, much of it across unwaymarked open moorland. He had not only walked this demanding route but backpacked too. I felt rather an inferior species of hiker in comparison. He recommended a material called moleskin for my sore feet and, once again, surgical spirit. The secret with surgical spirit is to apply it weeks before one's walk, to harden and dry out the feet in preparation .... I wish I'd known.

Thursday 10th May

The next morning my host dropped me off in Reading on his way to work and I had a cup of tea while I waited for the moleskin shop to open. Reading is not a town about which much that is flattering is said. Understandably. There are a few good buildings, even modern ones, but the overall effect is one of utter scrappiness. I found the Thames at Caversham Bridge beside the Headquarters of the Thames Conservancy. I descended to the towpath and followed the river to Tilehurst.

The houses on the opposite bank were large and luxurious – Reading seemed like an aberration. For the fourth day I was following the Thames and gazing at one desirable residence after another. It seemed that most people lived thus. Reading was different – the gas holders, the litter, the awful takeaway, the traffic, the stench. Of course the bulk of the population live in the Readings of England but it was easy, on this walk along the Thames towpath, to believe otherwise.

One is forced to leave the towpath at Tilehurst where, once again, it crosses banks at a ferryless point. I walked along the A329 and then bore down to the river at Mapledurham Lock. A pleasure boat passed me here and a woman called from it to ask where I was walking. I replied with studied nonchalance, "To Land's End"; she uttered an appropriate gasp and said she'd like to join me. Luckily her boat was chugging into the distance. Perhaps I'd have been better pleased if she'd offered me a lift up-river.

The countryside was lovely – flat meadows and the Chiltern Hills beyond. At Whitchurch I crossed the bridge and proceeded along the red brick main street, a world away from Reading. Now the Thames Walk follows an undulating course along farm tracks and paths through woods – this represented the edge of the Chilterns. The cut-off line was, of course, the river, which I could espy from time to time through a crack in the trees.

Reaching Goring at midday meant I had only walked about

11 miles but I planned to stay here overnight so as to be ready to begin the Ridgeway across the downs the following day. I had by now run out of friends to stay with. It had been pleasant to renew acquaintance in this way and I was grateful to them for offering me free hospitality in the otherwise expensive Thames Valley Region. Now I must find a billet for the night. First I had lunch - smoked mackerel and a pint in a pub across the river in Streatley – I had no more walking to do that day so felt I could indulge myself.

Opposite the pub was a Youth Hostel. I enquired about the possibility of staying there from a young woman working in the garden and she told me to come back later. In the meantime I made my way back to Goring and booked into a Bed and Breakfast establishment recommended in the RA Guide. I checked in, was shown my room and here I examined my feet – not a pretty sight – and applied strips of moleskin – the idea was that it should act as a second skin to sore parts of the feet.

I'd telephoned my wife earlier and moaned about my feet and suggested coming home and resuming my walk the following week but I knew it was impractical. Now I lay on my bed and thought about her and home and my three children. Of course I must continue my walk – an ambition I'd nursed for so long. I put on my sandals and shuffled back to Streatley. There I looked in at the Youth Hostel and met the warden who seemed enthusiastic I should join. I would have done had I not already booked in somewhere for the night. After a pub supper I spent an enjoyable evening going through the bookcase in the guest house lounge with my feet up.

Friday 11th May

Day 5 dawned .... today I would forsake the homely, familiar and inhabited Thameside footpath and climb the prehistoric track across the wide open Berkshire Downs. I shared my breakfast table with a middle-aged coach driver who was taking a party of school children from Dorset on a tour of the South Midlands. The previous day they had visited the Austin Rover works in Cowley, today they were going to Didcot Power Station. What a splendid way to show children from a rural backwater how the other half provides them with cars and electricity.

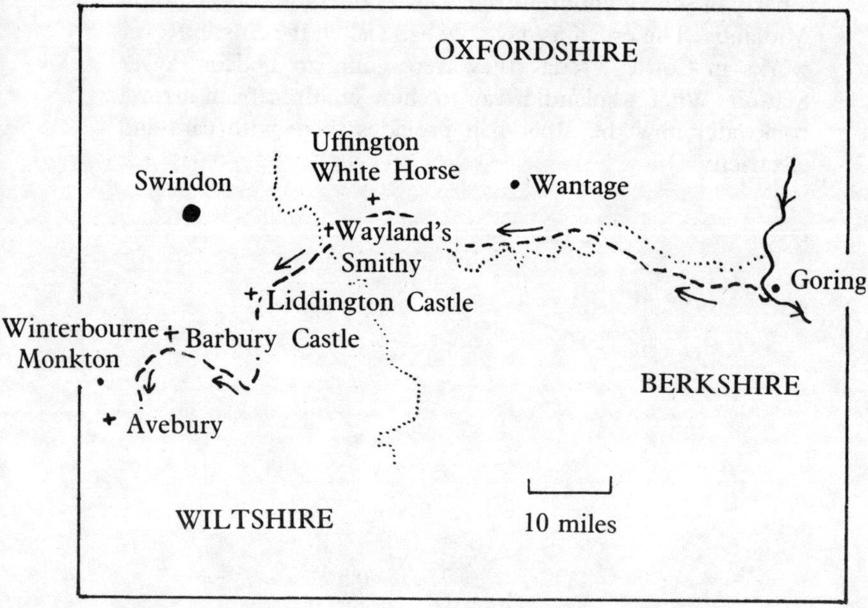

Along the Ridgeway

4 ALONG THE RIDGEWAY

With a massive breakfast inside me, my feet swathed in moleskin and new ground to break ahead of me, I set out hopefully, if not with a spring in my step. There is a final glimpse of the Thames from the climb towards the Ridgeway. The track to Warren Farm ends where the signposted Ridgeway begins. I was gaining height with each step. The sky was clear and there was a steady wind at my back which pushed me along. An immense view across the Vale of the White Horse suddenly opened up and the prospect of this ancient green road crossing the Downs ahead as far as one could see filled me with a tremendous sense of exhilaration, perhaps emphasised by the low point which I had reached the day before.

I was so absorbed that I missed a turning right below Blewbury Down and descended to East Ilsley. This was new ground and it was interesting to see the village and, a mile or two further on, West Ilsley, where sarsen stone is much used in the garden walls. These "sarsens", or foreigners, are found locally on the chalk downs and represent the resistant residue of a stratum of sandstone which once overlaid the chalk. I stopped for a pint of orange juice and lemonade in *The Harrow* at the western extremity of the village. The pub was packed with people drinking and eating great platefuls of food. I'd hardly seen a soul all morning and wondered where they could all have come from. The only concentration of people hereabouts likely to be having a pub lunch was the Atomic Energy Research Establishment a few miles to the north.

"An immense view across the Vale of the White Horse suddenly opened up"

I drank my pint quickly and did not sit down. A bridleway rejoined the Ridgeway at East Hendred Down and I plodded on for several miles. Beside the Ridgeway are many racehorse gallops with notices reminding walkers that they are private property and that mere humans should keep to the footpath. The Vale of the White Horse stretches out below the chalk scarp, the foreground scarred by the conglomeration of buildings at the Atomic Energy centre and, beyond, by the cooling towers of Didcot Power Station. The O.S. map gives the names of many hills and hollows along the Ridgeway. With the exception of the escarpment itself, one is hardly aware of these features on the ground. Rather there is the chalk upland, an endless arrangement of swellings and depressions on the one hand, and on the other the level clay vale. Whilst the upland is characterised by large arable fields, open grazing for sheep and copses of beech, the lowland is distinguished by a pattern of small fields and occasional villages.

I was aiming to end this day at Uffington where I hoped to find a place to stay. I barely stopped once between West Ilsley and Blowingstone Hill. After 20 miles my feet were nagging at me, notwithstanding the little relief afforded by the moleskin. I descended the hill and saw the Blowingstone in the garden of a cottage at the bottom. It is a sarsen stone riddled with holes like an outsize piece of gruyere cheese which, when blown in a certain way, emits a loud noise. Local legend has it that King Arthur summoned his armies for the Battle of Ashbury thus. Blowers on or admirers of the Stone are now asked to make a contribution to Kington Lisle Church.

I walked on to Kington Lisle, then across fields to Uffington. Whilst trying to search out the Bed and Breakfast establishment recommended in the R.A. guide I found another and knocked on the door. A young woman answered and welcomed me warmly, assumed I was walking the Ridgeway and showed me up to a spacious and comfortable room with books of local interest. She soon produced a large pot of tea which produced four mugsfull. I had walked a total of 23 miles on my poor shattered feet and lay on the bed for a long time. I eventually eased on my sandals and dragged myself to a local pub where I sat down to a delicious meal and a couple of pints of Morland's bitter.

I got back somehow and realised that I had left the pub without paying for my meal.

Saturday 12th May

After a hearty breakfast I set out for the Ridgeway, settling my debts on the way. Since leaving the Thames at Streatley I had been following the 1:50,000 O.S. map. The width of such maps represents, as the crow flies, around 25 miles. Maps of this scale are not detailed enough for exploring the intricate network of local footpaths in any given area but are adequate for following long distance footpaths and generally for finding a non-road route between two distant points. Together with the larger scale Pathfinder maps, I had been using the 1:50,000 Landranger Series for years to explore my local countryside and to devise circular rambles. On examining Sheet 174 I was astonished to discover that I had, the previous day, walked across almost three quarters of a 1:50,000 O.S. Sheet.

I ascended White Horse Hill and looked down on the Manger - a deeply penetrating, smoothly sculpted and most beautiful dry combe in the escarpment. The White Horse was, unfortunately, out of sight. I had visited it before; it is a remarkable disjointed figure of a horse, quite unlike all the other white horses cut into the chalk downs, most of which are no older than the eighteenth or nineteenth centuries. The Uffington White Horse does not attempt to be a realistic representation - it is an artist's impression but one that is evocative of a large galloping horse – full of power and grace. It dates from the first century B.C. or A.D. so is indeed an ancient feature of the landscape. It is best seen from the air, a fact which has given rise to some pretty wild theories about its origin.

I followed the lane around Uffington Castle until I reached the Ridgeway. The day was overcast but bright and when I reached Wayland's Smithy the clouds parted and the sun shone down. Saxon legend has it that Wayland, the divine blacksmith, would shoe your horse if a penny was left here. A somewhat more prosaic explanation is given on an official notice which reads: "A Neolithic Long Barrow built about 2000 B.C." The whole site is quite small, though complete and well maintained. It is surrounded by beech trees whose young green leaves shone brightly in the morning sun and cast flickering shadows on the ancient stones below. A few more miles led me across the county boundary from Berkshire into Wiltshire. Here I caught sight of Swindon through a gap in the hedge and hastily looked the other way.

In a couple more miles the path descends to a junction with the Ermine Street (Roman Road) at Foxhill. Here is a pub which is decidedly unfriendly to walkers. Notices debar walkers from the lounge, forbid "thick muddy boots" and instruct patrons to leave their rucksacks outside. I drank a pint of shandy and watched a party of cyclists play a game of pool, then left the pub and followed a minor road south-westwards across the M4 motorway below Liddington Hill, the place where the writer Richard Jefferies would retreat when he felt the need to commune with Nature:

> There was a hill to which I used to resort at such periods. The labour of walking three miles to it, all the while gradually acsending, seemed to clear my blood of the heaviness accumulated at home. On a warm summer day the slow continued rise required continual effort, which carried away the sense of oppression.

Jefferies lived at Coate Farm just south of Swindon and, in his younger days, worked as a reporter for the local newspaper.

The Ridgeway ceases to be a minor road and once again becomes a green track between fields. My feet were beginning to scream at me – I had walked about 15 miles since leaving

Wayland's Smithy: "the beech trees cast flickering shadows on the ancient stones"

Uffington and I had many more miles to go before reaching Avebury where I planned to spend the night. I kept myself going with the promise of a lie down and rest at Barbury Castle, a spot familiar to me from a day excursion I'd once made. The Ridgeway provided a gentle climb up the escarpment – a small mercy.

At a crossing point below the hill fort I dropped to the ground and eased off my shoes. I intended to doze off but was prevented by the incessant rip and roar of motorcycle engines. Young lads were testing their skills on a dirt track nearby and their machines sounded like a swarm of angry wasps, an infuriating sound which forced me to my feet once more. I plodded along the spine of Hackpen Hill with its panoramic views. A few miles further west the chalk escarpment finds an echo in the greensand escarpment, the two geological strata here separated by a kind of platform occupied by Avebury and neighbouring villages. Beyond the Vale of the White Horse I could just recognise the hazy blue outline of the Cotswold Hills.

I found these last few miles of the Ridgeway the most attractive of all. The views were immense - ahead to Morgan's Hill and Beacon Hill above Devizes and nearer at hand, the summit of Silbury Hill. The landscape seemed spacious and at peace, so much so that, even with the wretched state of my feet, I had a sense of rolling, or gliding, over the surface of the earth. To the east I could see the sarsen strewn Fyfield Down, now a nature reserve, the grey lumps of stone looking like a flock of sheep from this distance.

I finally left the Ridgeway and descended towards Avebury village. It was a Saturday and I had passed quite a number of walkers during the course of the day. I passed through the stone circles and concentric ditches within which the village is built. All the Bed and Breakfast establishments were full or at least so I was informed. Avebury is becoming quite a honeypot for tourists and no doubt the local landladies can fill their beds with clients more acceptable than walkers with their muddy boots and rucksacks and windswept hair.

Having exhausted all the possiblities in Avebury, I was given someone's phone number in the village of Winterbourne Monkton, a mile or two to the north. A phone call established that they would offer me bed and breakfast and evening meal. I dragged myself out of Avebury, having already mentally prepared to stay there. I suppose it took me a long time to reach Winterbourne Monkton and as I approached the village a middle-aged gentleman came striding towards me. He assumed I was his client and asked me if I smoked but without offering me a cigarette. I said no and he said good because he did not allow smoking in his house. Sure enough, as we arrived at the front door, there was a notice outside forbidding smoking inside.

I was offered a seat in a large lounge and given a cup of tea. I was later shown my room and took the opportunity to clean up. My hosts were extremely kind and inqisitive and I very much enjoyed the evening that followed. I shared their meal: a rather anglicised spaghetti Bolognese accompanied by some potent home-made wine and followed by home-made liqueur. We talked of all kinds of things: they had come to live in this tiny Wiltshire village upon retirement and leaving their home in London, had entered into the life of the community and clearly had no regrets about changing the metropolis for this rural backwater. They were Roman Catholics but, being far from a Catholic Church, had joined and played an active role in the local village church - a splendid example of the ecumenical spirit at work.

Sunday 13th May

My hosts' daughter and granddaughter were staying with them; the daughter was a nurse and the following morning she offered to look at my feet and give her professional advice. After a horrified stare she told me that the only chance they had of healing was for me to stop walking for a couple of days at least. They gave me animal wool to bind around my sore feet; I left Winternourne Monkton and set off back to Avebury. I'd not long waved my hosts goodbye when I decided that I would heed the advice offered and quit walking for a couple of days. It was Sunday; Avebury was as near as I would pass to my home in Bradford on Avon – if I was to reach Land's End and fully enjoy the rest of my walk it would be sensible to lie up for 48 hours.

I rang my wife on reaching Avebury and asked her to drive over and pick me up. I noticed that a service was about to begin in the charming little church of St. James; there were two baptisms during the service. I shuffled out of the church at the end of the service, shook hands with the young vicar and found my wife Hazel waiting for me in the porch – she had guessed my whereabouts.

In Bradford on Avon I felt greatly embarrassed at being seen only one week after setting out on my marathon walk. After Sunday dinner I visited the local hospital and had my feet attended to: the many blisters burst and drained, the tender toes bound to isolate them from the blackened toenails. The nurse asked me how they had got so bad - I felt a complete failure in telling her and also rather guilty about demanding N.H.S. resources for a self inflicted injury. I left the hospital, my feet bound in cotton wool, bandages and elasticated tubes - I could hardly pull on my sandals. At home I have never so much enjoyed sitting in an armchair for hours on end with my feet up.

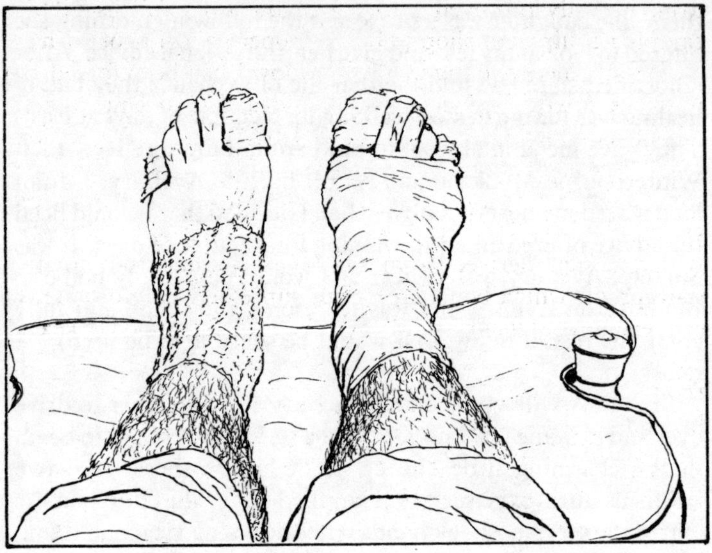

"I have never so much enjoyed sitting in an armchair for hours on end with my feet up"

Monday 14th May

The next day I removed all the dressings and my feet seemed to have greatly improved. I drove to Trowbridge and visited the camping equipment shop to buy a proper pair of boots. I had always shunned walking boots - but now I had been forced by bitter experience into accepting the idea. I tried on a pair of run-of-the-mill walking boots - they fitted like a glove and felt wonderful. In my enthusiasm the shop assistant encouraged me to try a much more expensive pair to see how much better they were. The very latest in boot technology, sir, ultralight, an Italian design derived from ski boots, perhaps not totally waterproof, which boots are? - but supremely comfortable, I can recommend them, sir. My feet slid in, I tightened the laces, stood up and walked around the shop. They were everything the salesman claimed, and more. They held my feet like the hands of some gentle giant and seemed to propel me forward with a little spring in every step.

I paid for them and took them home. A little more rest, a little mote healing and I felt confident about setting out again the next morning.

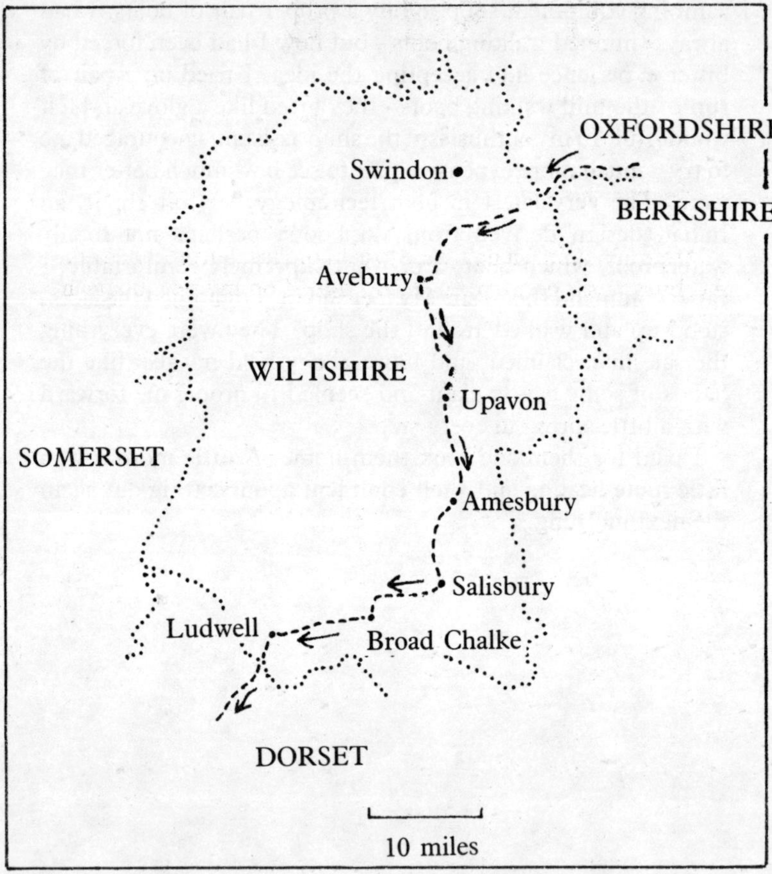

Round about Wiltshire

5 ROUND ABOUT WILTSHIRE

Tuesday 15th May

After my children had gone to school Hazel drove me back to Avebury. I sat on a sarsen stone, pulled on my new boots and strode off purposefully along the Stone Avenue. It was a fine day - a blue sky overhead and a gentle cool breeze - much as it had been when I'd set off from Chiswick eight days before.

The end of the Stone Avenue took me to West Kennett on the A4. I left the main road to follow the lane across the River Kennet, then quit the lane to follow a farm track to the southerly extension of the official Ridgeway Long Distance Path. This climbs the ridge between the Kennet Valley and the Vale of Pewsey; from here I could see Morgan's Hill and Beacon Hill to the west and the man-made Silbury Hill to the north. The dry combe below was littered with sarsen stones.

The Wansdyke is a linear earthwork which appears in two main sections - one south of Bath extending westwards into Somerset, the other on the Marlborough Downs from Morgan's Hill north of Devizes eastwards towards Savernake Forest. Opinion seems to be that the bank and ditch were dug by the Britons defending territory to the south against an Anglo-Saxon invader to the north. The Wiltshire section of the Wansdyke is now an officially designated public footpath and makes a splendid walk across the high ridge at the centre of the county. From the Wansdyke I descended the escarpment to the lane below Walker's Hill. This is a part of the Pewsey Downs

National Nature Reserve - a couple of miles to the east is West Woods, a Forestry Commission site which has many public rights of way.

Directly south of Walker's Hill I left the road to follow an old sunken path, marked on the O.S. map in Gothic script as "Ridge Way" and a way which I had used before. These secret paths have a special magic. It is perhaps surprising that the more one walks along footpaths, tracks, lanes and so on the more each one is remembered for some special, individual quality, though essentially all are really much the same. Perhaps it is a case of the more one sees of the same thing the more one notices the subtle differences that do exist. Another variable is of course the weather and the season. In high summer certain footpaths can become all but impenetrable - a tunnel of green from which one emerges as from a totally enclosed world. In winter the vegetation is stripped bare, the fields are empty, the flowers gone, the distances seem shorter and the bare bones of the landscape assert themselves.

The fascination of walking in the countryside springs from many things. Apart from the landscape itself, its shapes, colours and textures, its flowers and trees and birds and animals, its buildings and people, its underlying structure and shaping to man's needs, there are those man-made arteries of communication - the paths, the tracks and the lanes - each going somewhere different, each serving a different community and today, of course, much less used than they once were, a fact which only adds to their attraction. To walk them is to feel an intimacy with the land which is otherwise impossible - there are surprises around every corner, there are diversions at every step. To walk many miles in one day is to enjoy a constantly changing panorama. There are unexpected moments of drama, when one comes face to face with a fox, for example, or a disturbed pheasant flaps off in a sudden panic.

I remembered one of those dramatic moments which had occurred a few weeks earlier on my "practice walk" along the Wansdyke and through Pewsey Vale only a few miles from my present position. I was crossing a field when I heard a whining, much like a cat in distress. In the next field I found two animals jumping around together - one a rabbit and one a much smaller brown coloured creature. As I approached I could see that the rabbit was being attacked by a weasel – the latter had its jaws locked into the rabbit's throat. The weasel eventually leapt away into some trees; the rabbit was left panting and bleeding, a certain goner.

Dramatic moments of a different kind occur at the crest of a ridge when one looks back on one world and forward to another. My own addiction to footpaths has little to do with memories of idyllic childhood walks - I can remember but one walk: along the old railway track from St Aubin to Corbière in Jersey and apart from that, I can recall only endless solitary wandering across beaches and clambering over rocks. And yet I always seemed to have the idea in my mind of walking along paths and finding adventures. I remember staring hard at that compelling picture which was used to advertise Start Rite children's shoes: a boy and girl setting out along an endless road in new shoes - life's journey and all that! But perhaps a greater impression was made by the image of the Yellowbrick Road in *The Wizard of Oz* – an odyssey of childhood fears and their eventual conquest.

This old sunken path and the image of the Yellowbrick Road which it prompted led me to the twin villages of Alton Priors and Alton Barnes. I walked by the scattered buildings of Alton Priors to reach the church of All Saints, now redundant and locked and resting peacefully in a green field as though put out to grass like an old horse. A little further I crossed a footbridge over a tiny stream. This is the source of the Salisbury Avon which springs to life just a few yards to the north of this point where the chalk strata meet the impervious clay beneath. Either side of the bridge are turnstiles - an unusual and welcome sight. The right of way across the next field is marked by a line of sarsen blocks set in the turf which, I dare say, act as useful stepping stones in wet conditions.

Kennet and Avon Canal: "Here I dropped down onto the towpath and headed east for a mile or so"

Only a short distance from All Saints in the church of St Mary. I took a few minutes to look at this church which I had visited before and knew to date from Saxon times. On entering the building the tall, narrow proportions are most striking and instantly put one in mind of St Laurence in Bradford on Avon.

I walked away from the village and on to Honey Street, a former wharf on the Kennet and Avon Canal. Here I dropped down onto the canal towpath and headed east for a mile or so. The canal banks were full of growth and the surface of the water as smooth as glass except where disturbed by swans or moorhens. At the second bridge I left the canal and headed south through Woodborough, across the main line railway and along farm tracks until I emerged onto the main road at Manningford Bohune. I followed the road for less than a mile before bearing left along a lane which followed the left bank of the River Avon to Upavon.

On reaching the main road in the village I sat down on the verge to change maps and examine the route along the river. I had intended crossing the downs in a south-easterly direction from Manningford Bohune to reach Everleigh, and then to take the Old Marlborough Coach Road across the Army Firing Ranges to Bulford and Amesbury. However, the day was growing dull and rain seemed a distinct possibility. There were many peewits in the fields though I did not know if this was a sign of rain.

The lure of a river valley I had not much explored persuaded me to take the low road to Amesbury. Here I heard only the distant thud of the bullets and bombs on the Firing Ranges. I followed the minor road on the left bank of the Avon and, whenever possible, took short cuts using fieldpaths across water meadows and through the villages and hamlets of East Chisenbury, Fittleton, Netheravon (here I crossed to the right bank), Figheldean, Milston and Bulford to Amesbury. At Coombe there was a fine undershot waterwheel, still intact and, further on, a flint and chalkstone chequerwork wall.

In one of these places, and I cannot remember which, I

stopped by a roadside pub for a pint of shandy and a packet of crisps. What a pub! Three old men and an equally geriatric dog comprised the company. The conversation concerned the planting of runner beans and which was the most favourable time. The South Wiltshire accents and many dialect words were quite fascinating and I felt that this would be an ideal opportunity for those people whose task it is to record local speech. When I started on my crisps (the only "food" available) the old dog came and sat up on the bench next to me and stared at me most pleadingly.

It began to rain when I left the pub and rained steadily for the rest of the day – not a downpour, but a quiet, thin, steady, vertical drizzle – a dampening rather than a drenching rain and not unpleasant to walk in. It had been such a dry spring that the ground hardly noticed the rain and it was only in the lowest lying meadows, where the lady's smock grew, that it became at all squelchy underfoot.

I crossed the A303 by a footbridge and entered Amesbury. There were a lot of soldiers about. The time was getting on and I was considering the possibility of staying here, but didn't see anywhere that attracted me as I walked into town. By now I'd walked some 21 miles but felt I could carry on for a few more. The three miles from Amesbury to Great Durnford by tracks and field paths, up and over a low hill above the meandering Avon were most enjoyable in the wet twilight. As I emerged from the woods above Great Durnford I took off my waterproof overtrousers and tried to spruce myself up in anticipation of finding somewhere to stay.

Down in the village I enquired in the pub. The landlord did not know of anywhere locally but did recommend somewhere in the next village. He tried to phone through for me but the telephone had gone dead. I found the house in Netton, unmarked by a B & B sign, and rang the bell. A lady leaned out of an upstairs window and asked if I wanted to stay the night. I was shown my room and a sumptuous bathroom and given a radio. I thought I should eat first and crossed the river to the pub at Upper Woodford. One can imagine this enormous pub with its riverside garden packed to bursting on fine summer evenings but on this damp spring evening I was about the only person there and sat down to a generous plateful of mixed grill.

After an hour my feet felt a little tender when I got up to walk back to the village. The bath I enjoyed even more than the meal. This was followed by an application of surgical spirit and Mycil powder to my feet, the treatment recommended by the hospital in Bradford on Avon; this was to became a morning and nightly ritual.

Wednesday 16th May

The next day I sat down to what I can honestly say was the most extravagant breakfast I have ever enjoyed. My arrival had caused an upset in that the dining table had been laid with the silver service in preparation for a dinner party which was to be held the following evening. All this was cleared away - although I wouldn't have minded eating in the kitchen – and an astonishing array of crockery, cutlery, pots full of jams, marmalades, honeys, a choice of bread, cereals and so on and on. My landlady was an army wife who at first had been horrified when someone had turned up at her door asking for bed and breakfast (the previous owners had started the business) but had then accepted the idea and grown to enjoy it.

I bade my hostess farewell and started out towards Salisbury. I was relieved that my feet felt quite O.K. – I was confident that I'd got over the worst in the first six days and that my new boots and the fact that my feet were by now sufficiently hardened off would get me to Land's End quite happily. I continued along the lane on the left bank of the Avon through Salterton, Little Durnford, Stratford-sub-Castle (the Castle being Old Sarum) and on into Salisbury.

The rain had ceased in the night but the air was damp and clinging. The only sounds were the twittering of birds and the occasional bleating of sheep, the dominant view that of misty meadows punctuated by crack willows and seen through the drippy, overhanging trees beside the lane.

There seemed no question but that I should visit the Cathedral on my way through the city: that piercingly tall spire draws one like a magnet. When I arrived I was almost deterred from entering by the turnstile and entrance fee – like a municipal swimming pool! In the lavatories one is asked to make a contribution to their upkeep. I had a cup of tea and a home made cake in the cafe and took a long look at the cloisters and the Prisoners of Conscience window before departing. The latter I found quite incomprehensible but the cloisters at once becalming and welcoming and prompting feelings of peace within.

I left the Cathedral and headed south across the River Nadder, deeper and faster flowing than the Avon. The path is in the form of a causeway built across a low-lying meadow with the Cathedral half a mile to the east. The green meadow was lighted with lady's smock, buttercups and marsh marigold. I reached in turn the old mill on the south side of the watermeadow, St George's church in West Harnham, then headed south-west through a housing estate until I quite suddenly found an old green lane which I ascended towards the remains of a quarry. From here I could look back over Salisbury, all the detail lost in the day's murk, the Cathedral spire alone forming a deeper grey silhouette, the paler grey of the land and the sky merging together without definition.

The track I was following to reach the Old Shaftesbury Coach Road was as dry and as cracked as it must have been before the previous day's rain. The old road is barely wide enough for two coaches to pass side by side but makes an excellent footpath. It climbs out of Salisbury and follows a chalk ridge above the A39 to meet that road just below White Sheet Hill, a distance of some 16 miles. I planned to follow it for about half its length and to descend to the Ebble Valley at Broad Chalke.

The green road passes Salisbury Race Course (here a couple of golfers were pulling their trolleys) and much woodland appears on one side or the other. Opposite the Race Course was an encampment of travelling people – there was a distant blare of pop music and heaps of rubbish at the roadside. Beyond them was a site for both touring and permanently sited caravans, each correctly aligned in its own tidily fenced patch, a striking contrast to the previous settlement. I think, on balance, I preferred the tinkers' place – rubbish and noise seemed more natural than this land-consuming regimentation. I bought a pint of milk at the camp shop and set off past the wood known as Hare Warren.

The landscape was very quiet and without a ruffle of wind: it seemed as if the fields and trees were intent on absorbing the much needed rain that had fallen the previous day. The only interruption was an Army Land Rover which passed me first one way, then the other. Further on I passed a solitary Army truck which appeared to be a radio headquarters with its own generator in tow. Close by was a lone soldier speaking into a transmitter to someone called Roger, though apparently not me.

Owing to the dull and misty weather I had no clear view across the valleys to the north or south. On Compton Down I left the ridge-top road and headed downhill along a wide track flanked by beeches to the village of Broad Chalke which I understand is the home of our Nobel Prize winning novelist William Golding. I saw neither him nor anyone else. The rain started as I reached the lane and bore right, up the Ebble Valley, to Fifield Bavant. Wiltshire's smallest parish church stands here in a field opposite the few remaining buildings of a once much larger settlement. The Ebble was just a trickle; I was approaching its source.

At Ebbesbourne Wake I bought a pint of milk in the village shop and sat in the bus shelter drinking it. I walked on through Alvediston towards Berwick St.John. As I approached the latter the rain eased off and I could see across the fields to

Winklebury Hill, its summit marked by a fort. Beyond the source of the Ebble the country opens out into a wide expanse edged by hills giving something of the appearance of a giant amphitheatre. The Old Shaftesbury Coach Road could be seen a couple of miles to the north, the Ox Drove a couple of miles to the south, both clearly identified by a line of trees traversing their respective ridges.

I had not walked as far as the previous day but I felt rather tired. In the absence of any B.& B. signs I knocked on one or two doors but had no luck. I was told to go on to Ludwell. I began walking along the lane and thumbed a lift the couple of miles to the main road. The landlady at the B.& B. establishment in Ludwell was elderly, lived alone and was unwilling to take me, hoping that she might be approached by a man and wife which she would prefer. She told me to come back after I had eaten at the nearby pub and she would let me know. I waited a long time for the cook to arrive for a rather indifferent plateful of chili con carne and returned to my digs where the landlady reluctantly took me in. Only minutes after I had got into my room a couple arrived and were also taken in. The landlady presumably gave up her own bed.

Thursday 17th May

Breakfast was a contrast to the previous morning's. I won't go into detail but the egg and bacon were definitely sub-standard. My landlady told me about her grandson who had walked from Land's End to John O'Groats with a 56lb. pack; he was now in the army. The couple's car refused to start and as I walked away the man was anxiously looking out for the arrival of the A.A. van.

The day was again misty but perhaps not as dull as the previous two days. From Ludwell I headed south along a lane towards Ashmore Down and the Wiltshire/Dorset border. I was pleased to see a yellowhammer perched on a wire fence at the roadside. There is an intersection of roads at a high point from which the hills recede in deep folds. Such lonely crossroads seem incomplete unless accompanied by one or two cars, usually Sierras or Cavaliers, in which the drivers sit asleep at the wheel. Here was a roadsign indicating ways to Fontmell Magna, Blandford Forum and Melbury Abbas. I rolled those double-barrelled names around my tongue a few times. Dorset is surely the county which exceeds all others in exotic sounding place names.

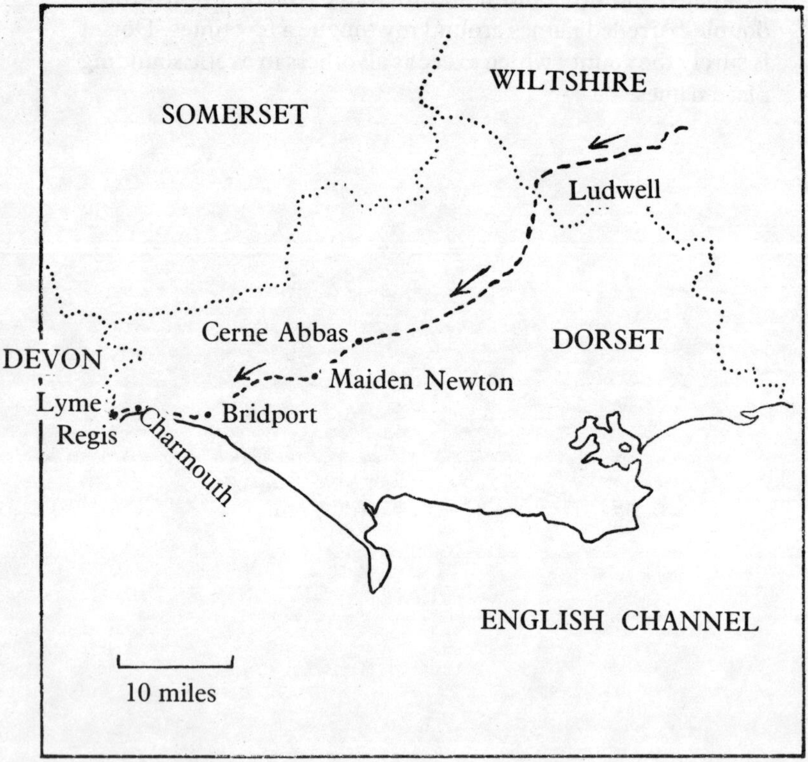

Through Dorset

6 THROUGH DORSET

I intended taking the lane to Ashmore and from there to head through the woods of Cranborne Chase, an area I was not familiar with. However, I took the wrong turning and found myself walking beside Compton Abbas Airfield to reach the minor road between Shaftesbury and Blandford. This lesser road follows the top of the chalk escarpment whilst the A-road runs along its foot. The scarp is deeply indented and faces the west in a series of swellings which I traversed as I headed southwards.

Now I left the road to follow a bridleway downhill towards Iwerne Minster, a large village on the main road betwixt Shaftesbury and Blandford. The chippings on the track were fragments of Carboniferous Limestone, from the Mendips no doubt, and foreigners in these parts. In Iwerne Minster I stopped for a pint of milk - I had certainly rediscovered the joy of milk. My father had been a milkman all his working life and it had been his habit to down a pint every morning after loading his barrow and before he set off on his deliveries. Milk is refreshing, cheap and of greater nutritional value than most drinks.

I followed field paths and lanes to Child Okeford. These were in part rather sunken in a sandy soil – here I was traversing the Greensand formation below the chalk. To the south is the chalk outlier of Hambledon Hill, with its fortified summit. As I crossed the River Stour I could see the tower of the church at Shillingstone, also to the south. In the valley here I passed

GRL-E

under the now defunct line of the Somerset and Dorset Joint Railway which once linked Poole and Bath and served the large rural area between.

At the beginning of a charming old track to Okeford Fitzpaine the sun broke through for the first time since Avebury. From Okeford the route led south-westwards along a lane at the foot of the chalk escarpment. I ascended the scarp by a gentle lane above Ibberton and carried on along the edge with tremendous views across Blackmoor Vale. The wind had picked up and that together with the intermittent sun had blown away a good deal of the mistiness of the previous two days. On Bulbarrow Hill a triangulation marker indicates a high point of 902 feet. There were pointers to various distant landmarks; Glastonbury Tor was 27 miles away but it was still not clear enough to see that great distance.

The wild flowers were a constant delight along this road: in a short stretch as I descended Bulbarrow Hill towards Anstey Cross I counted speedwell, herb robert, dandelions, red campion, jack by the hedge, white dead nettle, stitchwort, bluebells, sticky jack, yellow rattle, cow parsley, wild garlic and tufted vetch. I suppose mid-May is the climax of the wild flower calendar and for this reason alone a long distance walk across England can surely be taken at no better time.

The afternoon was drawing on and I had no clear idea where I might spend the night. The map showed that there was really no village between Melcombe Bingham and Cerne Abbas, some miles to the west. I was enjoying the Dorset Downs and decided to press on to Cerne, a place I had never visited.

I reached a farmyard beyond Melcombe where the cows were being let out after milking and I asked the cowman if I was right for the Dorsetshire Gap. He had a face straight out of a Thomas Hardy novel – a nut brown skin and black eyes. "Arrh! Dorsetshire Gap? Follow them cows, just follow them cows!" I was practically crushed to death at the gate ahead through which the herd was funnelled to reach the field. However I followed them cows across the field, along a ridge and into the next field. Before reaching the gap I sat down on the primrosy bank and gazed out over Blackmoor Vale in the evening light.

The Dorsetshire Gap pierces a narrow ridge of chalk and makes for interesting topography. Beyond the gap I traversed a field below a wood, crossed a lane and continued in the same general direction below Church Hill. I met a couple with a dog (which I saw first and mistakenly thought was a fox) and we fell into conversation for a pleasant mile. As we parted they gave me directions which I misinterpreted and resulted in my going a mile out of my way.

Darkness was approaching rapidly and I still had a good three miles to cover, another hour's walking, before reaching Cerne Abbas. From the Piddle Valley the grain of the land runs north/south which entails much upping and downing for someone heading east-west. As I descended towards Cerne Abbas I hoped that I would find somewhere to stay because I didn't think I could walk much further. The two B & B signs I spotted were at pubs. The first looked too posh, the second unpretentious and genuinely old-fashioned, the sort of establishment that the CAMRA Good Beer Guide would aptly refer to as a "basic town boozer". I asked at the bar and was shown up to a room lit with a 25 watt bulb. Beside twin beds the room also contained a rather Heath Robinson shower which I later found provided only cold water. After attending to my feet I padded down to the bar and ordered a trout. It was a superb meal and very good value which fact made up for the relatively expensive accommodation I was enjoying.

I was exhausted when I climbed into bed and yet I found it impossible to sleep. The pub owners seemed to spend hours watching a video in an adjacent room and a dog barked intermittently. When the video stopped and the dog was asleep there was a loud electric-sounding ping every minute or so. For what seemed hours this pinging continued. Quite suddenly I realised that it must be the shower head dripping onto the moulded plastic well at the base of the unit. I couldn't turn off the tap completely but placed a flannel under the descending drip to deaden the sound. On returning to bed I became conscious of another troubling noise – this came in short sharp bursts and sounded like a tape recording being played back fast – a kind of high-speed, high-pitched gibberish. Eventually I must have dozed off.

Friday 18th May

When I awoke I reached out to draw the curtains and noticed the continuous coming and going of a number of house martins, their movements interspersed with the sound of the tape recording – the noise was of course the chatter of these little birds. My remarks about the video and dog met with an apologetic response and was followed by the most enormous breakfast which I found impossible to finish.

From Cerne Abbas I set out west-south-westwards, over hill and dale, against the grain of the land. From Dickley Hill I looked back to Cerne and saw the Cerne Giant, eternally erect, through the haze. Over the top of Cowdown Hill and down to Sydling St Nicholas, embosomed in the downs, over Break Heart Hill and down to Maiden Newton. I was far from having an exact route in mind but knew that I wanted to hit the Dorset Coast round about Bridport. Making up a route using the 1:50,000 O.S. maps proved more interesting than following a long distance footpath like the Ridgeway. As I sat down to drink a pint of milk in Maiden Newton I noticed on studying the map that there was a disused railway line running from that village to Bridport. Although not designated a right of way, I determined to follow it.

I joined the old line beside the road out of Maiden Newton and followed it along a charming valley. I passed beneath the tiny settlement of Toller Fratrum, complete with chapel on the hill opposite, and walked on to Toller Porcorum ("Toller of the Pigs"). As I approached this last village I found that the trackbed had been incorporated into a number of back gardens. I asked a couple in Toller if it was possible to regain the railway line on the far side of the village; they gave me directions but were not certain how far it would take me. In fact it took me about another mile until it reached a road. Here it was obstructed with much barbed wire so I decided to try to locate a bridleway which ran through a wooded area indicated on the map as Powerstock Common.

As I entered the wood Powerstock Common turned out to be a nature reserve belonging to the Dorset Naturalist Trust and this bridleway provided a most delightful walk, through woods, beside ponds and across a heath which was carpeted with bluebells and flickering with orange tip butterflies - on this more open ground there was a splendid view south towards Eggardon Hill. A notice on the descent of the hill towards the edge of the reserve warned walkers to *Beware of Adders*. A lane led to Powerstock - a village picturesquely situated about a cleft beside the valley. Here I drank a pint of shandy and had a chat with the landlord in the pub. Now I found a footpath in the valley bottom to West Milton and emerged at its little redundant church.

From here I followed lanes, farm tracks and field paths into Bridport, a town I know and like very much and where I had hoped to stay at the Quaker Meeting House. I found the Meeting House Warden in her garden and introduced myself as a member of Bradford on Avon Meeting but was told that accommodation was not to be had. The Tourist Information Office was closed and the only B.& B. signs seemed to be outside pubs. Pubs do tend to be more expensive so I reluctantly decided to walk out of town on the main road west, reckoning that I would find somewhere along the way. I had just crossed the River Brit when I discovered Bridport Youth Hostel. The site of that green triangular Y.H.A. sign brought it all back to me – I hadn't stayed in a Youth Hostel for eighteen years or more.

I decided immediately that I would enquire whether I could

spend the night there. I met a young lady at the office and asked whether I was too old to join. She assured me that any age was a good age to join. So I did. I had to give her a cheque for the large sum required which included joining fee, hire of sheet sleeping bag, overnight charge, dinner and breakfast. It used to cost 3/6d per night but is now only slightly less than the cheaper end of the Bed and Breakfast market. Instead of the privacy of one's own room one shares a bunk in a dormitory. Sharing and community is what Youth Hostels are about – in this respect I found that they had not changed at all from what I remembered. One still has to perform a morning duty. In fact I had a dormitory to myself. There was a school party staying but all the boys and male teachers were together elsewhere. At dinner I sat with the kids and enjoyed talking to them. One told me I was mad to be walking to Land's End - "What, not even hitch hiking?"

Saturday 19th May

The next morning I set out with eager anticipation – the Dorset coast path between West Bay and Beer I knew pretty well and rated highly for walking enjoyment. I stepped out of Bridport along the charming South Street, then turned off right by Palmers Brewery, over the River Brit, and across fields and meadows beside the meandering river. I crossed a stile to enter the grounds of a large municipal camping and caravan site and availed myself of the excellent toilet facilities provided. It was a superb day – though visibility still rather marred by a clinging haze – a gentle sun, and a light cool breeze which came from the north east but which barely disturbed the glassy sea....conditions ideal for walking.

The sign-post at Eype Mouth indicated '2 miles and 1½ hours' to Seatown. Such was my enthusiasm that I did it in forty minutes and found the toes of my boots quite yellow from the buttercups through which I had been kicking over the clifftops.

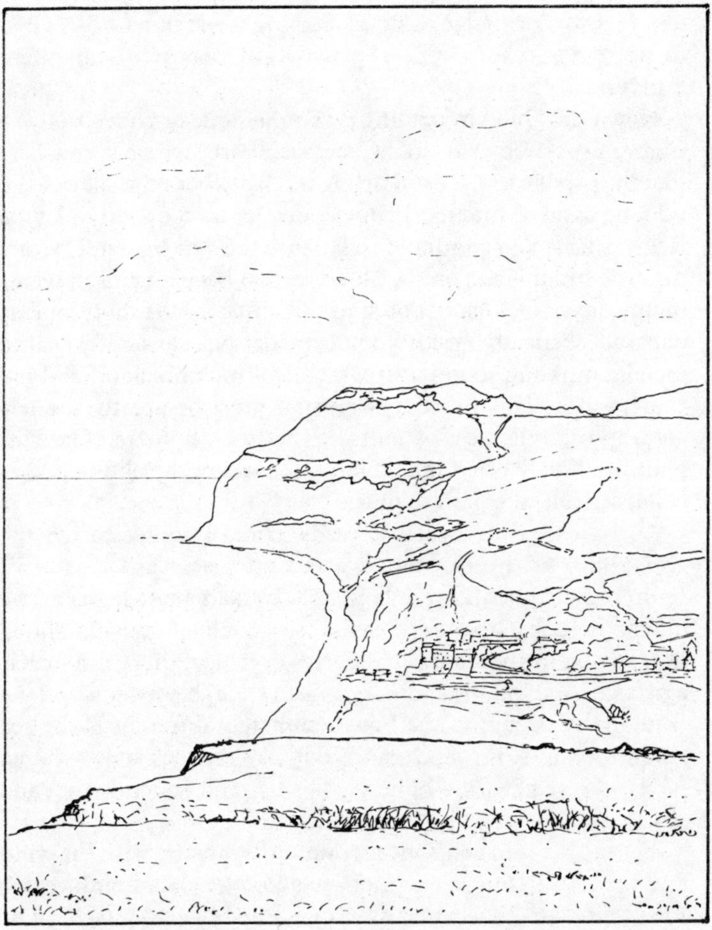

Golden Cap on the Dorset Coast Path: "It was a superb day – a gentle sun and a light cool breeze which barely disturbed the glassy sea"

At Seatown and recalled our first camping holiday here about 11 years previously when our twin boys were two years old. The tent blew over a hedge as I was erecting it and our toddlers had to be tethered to a tent peg with guy ropes to stop them wandering off.

Now I delighted in striding down the slope of Cain's Folly to Charmouth. We had spent several short holidays at Charmouth. I spoke to the Car Park Attendant about the state of the tide; he assured me that I could safely cross the sand to Lyme Regis. Black Ven continues to fall into the sea: the sandy strata near the summit rest on the blue-grey lias beneath and all seems highly unstable. Glaciers of mud spill out over the shore and, as one walks beneath the cliffs on a calm day one constantly hears a metallic tinkling sound as fragments of rock break off and fall beachwards. This process of erosion must be greatly accelerated by the relentless assaults of the fossil hunters. The cliff path itself is diverted inland at points where the cliff edge has collapsed and the path with it.

As I crossed the beach towards Lyme I contemplated the cliffs, the beach, the tiny waves, the backwash, the sea's sculpting of the sand, the land at one hand and the sea at the other. Perhaps because I spent so much of my childhood holidays on the beach, nearly always in Jersey, the sea shore has a particular fascination for me. It is to state the obvious and yet it regularly occurs to me how completely different is the sea from the land – the land stands out, asserts itself, takes shape, whilst the sea fills the hollows, lies flat and conceals the land beneath.

Yet the sea is in constant motion, in sympathy with the wind and the moon, and in this motion is forever claiming the earth for itself, for concealment within and beneath itself. The meeting place of these two basic elements of our planet, the shore, is literally at the edge of two worlds, of earth and of water. Of the other two elements, air and fire, air covers all invisibly, whilst fire transforms solids to gas and dust, the former to join the air, the latter the earth. Of the four elements then, earth and water seem to be the most basic, and the sea shore is their meeting point.

Lyme Regis is surely one of the most delightful towns on the south coast of England. I walked along the promenade, above the sandy beach and towards the Cobb or harbour and spent a pleasant half hour browsing and chatting in the second-hand bookshop. From here I had to climb up the steep hill to reach the huge car park on the main road to Exeter. It is from the south west corner of this car park that one finds the beginning of the coast path from Lyme to Seaton through the Axmouth Undercliff and from Dorset into Devon.

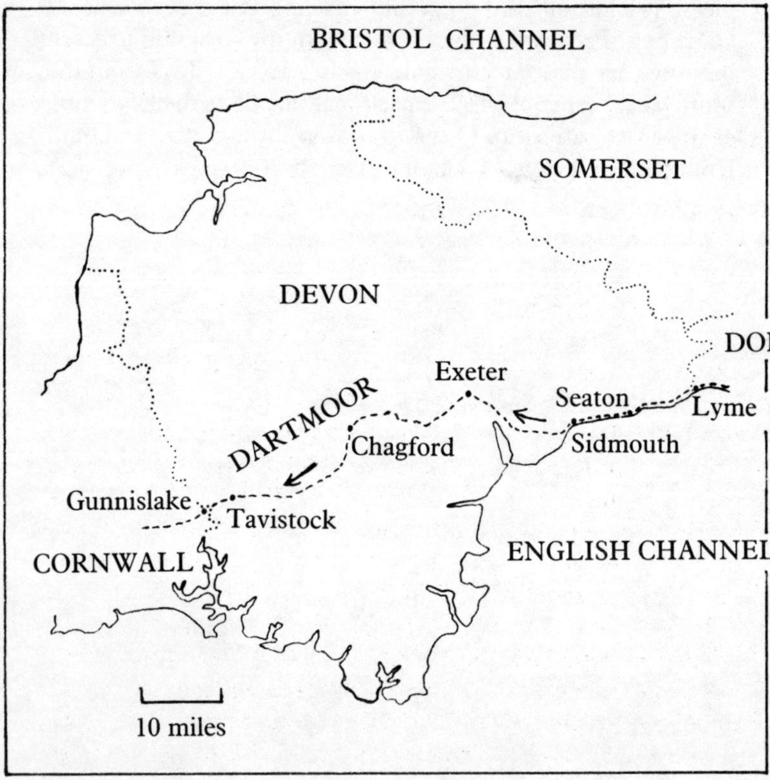

Across Devon

7 ACROSS DEVON

I had done this walk the year before with my wife and daughter. I was pleased that our eighteen-month-old had walked much of the seven miles. The footpath here winds its way through a completely wild and unspoilt landscape of broken cliffs: here the rock strata dip towards the sea so that the cliffs are inherently unstable. There was an enormous fall in 1839 when some 40 acres subsided towards the sea, tearing a chasm half a mile long and from 130 to 210 feet deep. Heavy rainfall had caused the Cretaceous strata above the Triassic marl to slip down towards the sea. This movement caused a corresponding ridge to be thrust up some distance out in the sea – this was quickly eroded by the action of the waves, and the broken cliffs and chasms were rapidly colonised by a wide variety of trees and plants.

In following the path it is interesting to observe how one species predominates for a short stretch but is soon overtaken by another. In such a confused landscape soil conditions and drainage vary greatly – this no doubt has an important bearing on the number and occurrence of plant species to be found. At one step dog's mercury predominates, then wild garlic, now hart's tongue fern. The trees clamour for the maximum sunlight and all are hung with myriad creepers.

I suddenly emerged from the green tunnel of the Axmouth Undercliff on the cliff top about a mile east of the River Axe and seaside town of Seaton. Descending to river level I crossed the bridge beyond which the sea has all but dammed the river's mouth by heaping up a great mound of pebbles. I followed the coast path out of Seaton, up and over cliffs towards Beer. As I walked through the streets I noticed a lot of cars with "I Love Beer" stickers in their back windows and did not immediately link this with feelings of local patriotism but rather a passion for ale. I found the Youth Hostel and after washing my feet was told it was full with a coach load of schoolchildren who had arrived unannounced.

Feeling rather less sentimental about the Y.H.A. than I had the previous evening I dragged myself back into town and checked into one of the numerous B.& B. establishments at which the landlord seemed quite used to accommodating the overflow from the Youth Hostel. Once cleaned up I visited a recommended pub and enjoyed my meal (chili con carne again). The sight and sound of the clientele reminded me most forcefully that I was now in Devon. I had lived in Newton Abbot for four years and learned to recognise a South Devon accent at a hundred yards – it's a very distinctive variety of West Country accent which is not forgotten once you have grown accustomed to it. The faces too were familiar – red and round and kissed by the sea breezes.

Sunday 20th May

The following morning I shared breakfast with a strapping German girl, a student teacher, who thought England tedious, "all green fields and hills and hedges" and France a far more varied and beautiful landscape. I started out to walk the coast path to Sidmouth, only a small section of which I had covered before. I went a good mile out of my way to the end of a large housing estate and back again before I eventually found my way up onto Beer Head. This marks the most westerly outcrop of chalk on the south coast and provides a spectacular scene. A coast guard lookout marks this windswept spot and the views down to the beach and toward Branscombe are superb and awe inspiring.

Beer Head

The descent to Branscombe Mouth is very steep. It was a fine day and two hardy souls were taking a dip. The climb out of Branscombe Mouth was as steep as the climb down but, thankfully, the coast path did not lead me to the cliff summit but "around the back" above a valley from which I could look down upon Branscombe Church. Now that I had left the chalk behind there seemed to be more bracken and hart's tongue fern, generally speaking a more luxurious undergrowth in the woods beside the path. Whereas cow parsley had been the most commonly observed wild plant before I reached Devon – every lane seemed to be fringed with a waving ribbon of it - now the most frequent was angelica: less delicate in appearance but somehow more lush, more exotic, less English. I also spotted a tiny, brilliant blue butterfly, most likely the Common Blue.

From Weston Cliff I could see Sidmouth in the distance and the lesser cliffs which lead westward to Budleigh Salterton. At the mouth of some insignificant stream I was once again at sea level. Here I was deterred from scaling Dunscombe Cliff by the sight of its very steep flank. I trudged on along the shingle beach but this was almost equally hard work. The cliffs are built of layers of the vivid red rocks that are typical of South Devon. The startling redness is alleviated by occasional bands of grey marl and haphazardly arranged veins of calcite, known to the quarrymen as "beef", on account of their fibrous structure.

At the next inlet, Salcombe Mouth, I climbed up to the cliff top, a climb that in places was so steep that I was forced onto all fours. I found the cliff paths between Beer and Sidmouth the most demanding section of my entire walk. It beat anything along the North Cornwall Coast Path. As I began to descend from Salcombe Hill Cliff I gained an enormous view over Sidmouth and Sidford. As at Seaton and the mouth of the Axe, the River Sid is sealed off from the sea by a storm beach. Not finding a shop open (only later did I realise it was Sunday) I looked quite hard for a pub in this sedate resort. Eventually one appeared advertising food with "local bread" - an unusual claim to authenticity. When I emerged I found that the sky had clouded over and the wind picked up.

I walked along the coast path, through a pine forest, as far as Ladram Bay with its impressive and rather menacing stacks of blood red sandstone standing just offshore like sentries on guard. At this point I forsook the coast path and the sea - not to be encountered again until Padstow. I walked through the pleasant streets of Otterton, the sizeable "ton" beside the River Otter. This was typical Devonshire: a long street of colour washed cottages - white and pink predominantly - with black skirts and thatched roofs. At Otterton Mill I had a pot of tea and a hunk of wholefoody- looking cake. Everything had dates or figs or walnuts in it – here were no sponges clad in sugar icing and topped with glacé cherries. People were prodding these dark-coloured, high-fibred specimens with some suspicion and selecting the least unfamiliar looking piece .... we are so used to refined and artificially coloured food.

Crossing the line of the former branch railway to Budleigh Salterton I passed the old Otterton Station and pressed on through East Budleigh. As I was walking along a lane past the village a herd of Guernsey cows came towards me – Guernseys are noticeably larger beasts than Jerseys. As they were passing me one of the herd, who had rather darker colouring than the rest, reared up in alarm. The farmer, who followed behind in a Land Rover, identified the shy individual as "Laurel". I was delighted that the farmer not only knew particular characteristics of members of his herd but had also given them names. He liked Guernseys, the farmer explained, although Jerseys gave very good butterfat.

There was a lot of borage in the hedgerow hereabouts – I always enjoy the pure blue colour of wild borage – as pure as the sky. I passed by Hayes Barton – the birthplace of Sir Walter Ralegh – now a hotel serving afternoon teas. Soon I reached a high point on the heathy commons of this part of East Devon. This rather poor, sandy soil sustains the usual mixture of pine and silver birch and gorse. Quantities of violets grew

"A herd of Guernsey cows came towards me"

beneath the trees on the roadside. I missed a right turning along a track over Lympstone Common and came down onto the busy Exmouth – Exeter road above Lympstone, with its view of the Exe estuary and the Haldon Hills beyond.

It was beginning to rain and, as there was no alternative route to the Youth Hostel at Countess Wear south of Exeter I decided to thumb a ride. In this I was unsuccessful – it was Sunday and nearly all the passing vehicles were cars full of families returning from a day out at Exmouth. I eventually caught a bus which took me around Topsham and dropped me off about half a mile from the hostel.

One of the pleasures of youth hostelling is found simply in visiting the hostels themselves. They are all so different one from another. Bridport hostel is situated in what was once a flax warehouse and ropeworks, whilst Beer's is a former private house of singular appearance standing in its own landscaped grounds. Exeter's is a large, mainly purpose-built hostel overlooking the River Exe on the southern outskirts of the town. I checked in and enjoyed a chat with the young wardens. They asked me if I would like supper and told me to join them in the kitchen later on. When I did I was given a plate of chili con carne – for the third time in five days!

Monday 21st May.

I set out next morning from the Youth Hostel and crossed one after the other the River Exe, the Exeter Canal and the main line railway. The Exeter Canal is interesting in being the oldest ship canal in the country, having first opened in 1564. The railway is interesting in that Brunel chose to run the line along the coast in order to overcome the obstacle of the Haldon Hills; it was opened in 1846 and ran between Exeter and Newton Abbot on the atmospheric principle, - a continuous pipe was laid between the tracks in which a vacuum was created by power supplied by engine houses built beside the track at intervals. Within the tube the vacuum drew a piston which was connected with the train through a vertical driving rod. A leather flap provided a longitudinal opening along the length of the pipe but this proved highly unreliable, being subject to attack by rats and the corrosive effects of the sea air. This unlikely scheme was one of Brunel's greatest failures and the line was converted to steam after 12 months. The only reminders of the original system are the pumping station tower at Starcross on the Exe estuary and some of the piping used for drainage on the beaches around Dawlish.

I was happy to quit the main road on the far side of the estuary. I intended to follow winding lanes via Shillingford St George due west until I reached the river Teign at Bridford-mills, then to follow the river upstream as far as Chagford. The O.S. map indicates a Nature Trail along the Teign Valley from Steps Bridge for several miles.

I could not find the footpath which would have provided me with a short cut at Alphington and was forced to walk into that village and out again. I crossed the A30 and finally felt I had left Exeter behind and had quite suddenly entered the rural heart of Devonshire. The lanes were exceedingly quiet, probably a good deal quieter than many long-distance footpaths. I could see ahead to the forest-clad Haldon Hills. Often the hedges were so high that one could not see the view – here there were always the wild flowers and the occasional gate into an adjacent field. In one very deeply incised lane I spotted a baby rabbit, so small that he would have had room to spare on the palm of my hand. I noted that he was about the size of a tennis ball. He froze as I approached, no doubt hoping not to be noticed. I certainly noticed him and found him quite irresistible. He was evidently lost: too small and weak to clamber up the steep banks – he had perhaps forgotten how he'd arrived at that spot.

At the side of the lane was an outcropping of slate. One always thinks of the red rocks of South Devon and of the granite of High Dartmoor, yet it is the grey slate of the geological formation named after the county – the Devonian – which is the most typical rock of Devon. Here I saw a wild flower which I did not recognise. My notebook records that it was around ten inches tall; its flowers white but purplish inside, something like an antirrhinum but the flowers sprouting directly from the stem and with leaves like those of a stinging nettle, but I have been unable to identify it since.

Windy Cross is well named: it is high up and exposed in a westerly direction towards Dartmoor – here one emerges from a much wooded country. The moss on the slaty rocks at the roadside indicated a damper climate.

From Dunchideock to the Teign, a distance of around 5 miles, no cars overtook me; I passed only two people on horseback and a herd of South Devons – cows, calves and one bull. There was a purple orchid in the hedgebank and the goosegrass was in flower which it had not been further east. I walked under an old railway bridge – the former line from

Chudleigh to Exeter once passed this way. This provided an alternative to the route along the coast between Exeter and Newton Abbot and I now crossed the B3193 and continued towards a farm where the map showed there to be a right of way beside the Teign towards Dunsford.

Beyond Dunsford I was attracted by a roadside notice advertising fresh strawberries for sale. I bought a punnet but was disappointed to find they were imported from France. A carton of banana flavoured milk completed this unDevonian lunch. Further on a roadsign indicated the proximity of the Royal Oak Inn and its provision of "Real Food and Real Ale" – an odd comment on our times. Approaching Steps Bridge I overtook a herd of sheep which were being urged forward, but without much success, by a brace of sheepdogs, the farmer's wife bringing up the rear in a tractor.

At Steps Bridge I passed the time of day chatting with the lady in the National Trust Information Point and the warden of the nearby Youth Hostel who happened to be passing with his binoculars. He had been spotting wildlife but had not seen any otters, those elusive creatures of the wild which I had never clapped eyes upon. The riverside footpath beside the Teign is an official Nature Trail and is well used by visitors to the National Park. It runs for many miles via Clifford Bridge and Fingle Bridge and links up with the Two Moors Way just below Castle Drogo. The Way is an unofficial long-distance footpath which runs from Lynmouth in North Devon, through Exmoor, across mid-Devon and over Dartmoor from Drewsteignton to Ivybridge. I followed the Way for a couple of miles to Rushford, there crossing the river to reach Chagford.

The Nature Trail from Steps Bridge is a delightful and attractive route if perhaps a little claustrophobic. The Teign cuts quite a gorge through these northern slopes of the moor and the valley sides are for the most part well wooded. The river is peaty brown, though very clear and is, in this respect, typical of Dartmoor streams. The Trail was busy with walkers. I encountered a greater concentration of people between Steps

Bridge and Fingle Bridge than anywhere else on the whole length of my walk from London to Land's End except possibly the final Bank Holiday Sunday as I approached the End.

At Fingle Bridge, a much frequented beauty spot, I stopped for a cup of tea and sat to gaze at the old granite bridge which is reckoned to date from the 16th or 17th century. When I set off once again I was following the Teign through the Drogo Estate. The riverside footpath has been replaced, whether for reasons of conservation or for the privacy of fishermen I know not, by a new path which undulates between river level and around 60 feet and does serve to provide some varied vantage points. At one point the path skirts a large outcrop of granite; here I saw my first pennywort, one of my favourite wild plants and one that speaks eloquently for the rain and rock of the West of England. On joining the Two Moors Way I left the woods and traversed a riverside meadow lighted with bright buttercups. This was a sudden and complete change of scene after the miles of steep and wooded river valley.

At Dogmarsh Bridge I left the Drogo Estate and entered woodland once more, then open meadow again. Chagford now became visible, the little town dominated by its church tower. At Rushford Mill I crossed to the southern bank of the Teign by some delightful stepping stones, then followed the road past the welcoming sign, "Chagford – Ancient Stannary Town, 1305 A.D." The nearest Youth Hostel is at Gidleigh, some three or four miles distant and not on my path. I found a good bed and breakfast and, after the performance with surgical spirit and Mycil Powder stepped out to view the town.

Chagford means "gorse ford" from the old dialect word Chag meaning gorse; locals tend to pronounce it "Chaggiford". A granite bridge was built here before 1224 and in 1305 Chagford was made a stannary town where tinners must bring their metal for coinage. By the end of the sixteenth century the spinning of wool for the East Devon weaving towns overtook tin as a source of the town's prosperity but declined in the early 1800s. The railway never reached Chagford, although a carriage and later a

"I crossed to the southern bank of the Teign by some stepping stones"

motor bus linked the town with Moretonhampstead and the branch line to Newton Abbot. From the turn of the present century, Chagford has grown as a residential and tourist centre though, happily, it has by no means entirely prostituted itself to the demands of the retired and the itinerant, like so many other places in the county.

Chagford was the furthest flung outpost of the Newton Abbot Division of Devon County Library for which I had responsibility as divisional librarian from 1976 to 1980. The library had been housed in a tiny room at the back of the village hall – I checked it was still there, indeed it was. I enjoyed the drive out from Newton Abbot and more than once nearly ploughed through a stone wall as I looked hard at some hanging wood or distant tor. Chagford is far enough away from larger centres of population to have maintained a self-sufficiency and variety of shops which give it real character and interest. The pubs, too, are several and varied. I settled for the one which my landlady recommended, a great barn of a place and busy with visitors and locals alike (the presence of the latter always a good sign) and ordered a drink and a meal from a rotund and red-faced landlord.

Tuesday 22nd May

This particular itinerant left his warm and comfortable digs at 9.00am and walked through the little town. It was raining steadily and blowing moderately but I felt pretty well protected in my walking boots, oiled jacket and rainhat. I soon found a public footpath sign indicating a right of way across a sloping field which provided a more direct route than the lane. Having kicked through a couple of grassy fields I could feel the damp penetrating my boots and two layers of socks. When I regained the lane I stopped to pull on my waterproof overtrousers.

The symmetrically proportioned Meldon Hill was on my right; the lower slopes consisting of arable land but higher up the hill was wild and rock strewn. Again I left the metalled road to follow a more direct way south, passing a farm called Yellands - a common place name in Devon and Cornwall meaning “old lands”. As I strode downhill past the farm in the pouring rain I saw an old man leaning on his stick and staring out from the open doorway of an adjoining barn, a sack pulled around his shoulders. I saw him before he saw me and he seemed a little startled by my appearance. We exchanged greetings and I began climbing out of the valley to the road at Yellands Cross. In another mile or so I gained height and entered into the open and unenclosed hinterland of Dartmoor. I passed a Devon County Council Highways lorry and a couple of men attending to something at a cattle grid. They were clad from head to foot in yellow plastic and looked like a couple of trawlermen. “You’ve chosed a lovely day to go hiking”, said one of them.

Approaching the Moretonhampstead-Tavistock road the rain was neither falling steadily, nor pouring, but lashing down with the aid of a fierce gale which did not blow from one direction but buffeted me ceaselessly from every side. By this time I was indeed very wet – my feet were squelching in my boots, my legs felt very damp in spite of my allegedly waterproof overtrousers and the rain had got between my hat and jacket collar and soaked my neck and shoulders. My spectacles were difficult to see through but I was comforted by the thought that I had at last reached the main road across the moor and the Warren House Inn, that lonely refuge of travellers on Dartmoor, was less than two miles away.

My plan for crossing Dartmoor was to leave the road at Postbridge and then to follow rights of way via Bellever Tor, Dunnabridge, the River Swincombe and the woods around Burrator Reservoir as far as Yelverton or Buckland Monachorum to enter Cornwall at Calstock. On reaching the main road I knew that I would have to abandon this plan and, quite frankly, to get to some place out of the rain as soon as possible. I was wet and cold and I began half-heartedly to thumb a ride. Not surprisingly, there wasn't much traffic – a few delivery vans, one or two cars, fewer lorries and a number of coaches on holiday tours, colourfully painted and bearing names like *Sunnyway Tours of Wigan*. There is no such thing as a sheltered spot on the B3212 and I trudged on to the Warren House Inn, which I really rather wanted to visit before giving up on Dartmoor and the day's walking. It was all I could do to keep upright as I picked my way along the grass verge, the blast was so intense.

At last a grey shape loomed out of the storm by the roadside ahead - the *Warren House Inn*. I had driven past it many times during the four years I had lived in Devon but never once visited it. I had rarely been so relieved to see a pub! But would it be open? It was not yet 11 o'clock and the landlord would surely not rush to open up on a day such as this - unless he were expecting an influx of defeated walkers like myself.

From the storm porch of the inn I crossed the road and thankfully saw a light inside. I took off my rainhat and rucksack – now a sodden lump – and deposited them on the stone seat there. Inside was a blazing log fire and two barmen apparently much amused. I told them I had walked from Chagford – about seven miles – and that conditions were not at all bad when I left Chagford but had grown steadily worse as I approached the high moor. As I spoke to them I caught a delicious aroma of coffee and ordered a cup. I had considered asking for a brandy too but thought better of this rather melodramatic gesture. I sat down beside the roaring fire and began to steam. I asked about buses – I remembered the minibuses that went under the name of the *Dartmoor Pony Express* - surely they would be working. Not for another six weeks, I was told. There was no one else in the pub to ask. There seemed nothing for it but to hitch.

The *Warren House Inn* is strategically sited on the south side of a hill so I was protected from the worst of the blast as I waited for a lift. As it happened the first car that came along stopped and an elderly gentleman in tweeds got out to open the boot for my rucksack. He drove slowly and carefully to Tavistock and we conversed together all the way. Having trained to work in the Canadian paper industry, the company he was to join went bust in the Depression. He had subsequently had a career as an army scientist which he had enjoyed. My driver was on his way to a friend near Tavistock while staying on the far side of Dartmoor. He couldn't remember the name of the place where he was staying – I hope it came back to him later in the day because he didn't seem too sure of the roads.

It was raining hard in Tavistock and everything was dripping and the roads and pavements full of puddles. I like Tavistock – I like the sound of the name and I love that dark sea-green stone from which the town is built. It is actually a volcanic ash known as Hurdwick Stone and is worked in quarries a mile or two north of the town. It is highly individual and reminds me more of the Buttermere slate of the Lake District than any other rock in Devon or Cornwall. It looks best when wet so today it looked magnificent. My host dropped me in the square flanked by the stately town hall and the three-gabled church of St Eustace. It was just midday and I was looking forward to drying out and having a look round Tavistock where I knew there were some secondhand bookshops.

My O.S. map showed a Youth Hostel but my 1984 Handbook did not list it – it had evidently closed. There was one entry in the RA Bed and Breakfast Guide for Tavistock. I eventually located it some way from the centre of town only to find it full. I wondered if I'd deterred the landlady with my dripping wet clothes and tried to excuse my appearance and the fact it was so early in the day to be looking for accommodation. She assured me that she would take me if she were not full with people staying for the Ten Tors Expedition, the annual trek around the ten highest Dartmoor peaks which was taking place that weekend.

I made my way back to town, now completey drenched, and went into a public loo to try and tidy up. I took off my rainhat and was shocked by my reflection in the mirror. I'd had my hat jammed down on my head all morning. The rain had penetrated the hat and my ample hair was moulded into the shape of the hat - flat against the side of my head, sticking out around the collar with a kind of high wedge on top.

Back in town I enquired at the Tourist Information Bureau about accommodation. I was told that there were several Bed and Breakfast establishments on the Plymouth Road not far away. The first one I tried was full (Ten Tors) but the second took me in. It was a large Victorian house and I suppose was the most "commercial" place I had stayed in, apart from the pub at Cerne Abbas, though not expensive. I asked about drying facilities and was shown an electric convector heater on the landing outside my room. What luck!

Everything was wet, including the contents of my rucksack, so even if I had had a change of clothes they would have been no use. A lesson for the future: place any dry clothing, etc., in plastic bags before packing in rucksack. All I could find that was not more than damp was my pair of shorts. I could hardly sit in the lounge downstairs in nothing but a pair of shorts so, having draped my wet clothes on chairs to make best use of the 1 kilowatt of heat I retreated to bed. Here I was dismayed to find nylon, not cotton, sheets which were not only nylon but turquoise in colour and much snagged by the broken toenails of countless former occupants. I crept out onto the landing about an hour later to turn my clothes which were drying nicely. I reckoned they'd be sufficiently aired by 3 o'clock to dress and go out.

It was still raining heavily when I walked to the shops in my still damp clothes. The first thing I must do was to buy an umbrella. I went into a pleasingly old-fashioned shop to select a brolly; the cheapest were automatic and, I thought, easily broken. The nicest ones had leather handles, were British made and very expensive. I settled for the cheapest manual variety which was in traditional black and rather handsome. I felt a new man as I ambled down the street completely protected from the downpour.

The large second-hand bookshop that I remembered from a previous visit had apparently closed down following the death of its owner. I visited another and spent more time talking with the proprietor than I did browsing, as I did in a nearby curio shop where the owner asked me where I was from and insisted on showing me his collection of old postcards of Wiltshire. I thought I had already looked through these but he explained that he kept the best ones under the counter. I found a view, *circa* 1900, of the street in Bradford on Avon where my shop is situated. I also found a very nice one of a clappergate stile at Charlecote (now spelt Chalcutt), a village near Calne. When I expressed an interest in stiles, the shopkeeper dug into the Cornish section to find an old coloured postcard depicting a lady in long skirts approaching a Cornish stone stile. These three discarded scraps of paper added up to £3.50 which the shopkeeper generously reduced to £3.00. I'd never bought old postcards before and hadn't imagined I could spend that much on them.

I walked around all the shops and had tea and a piece of treacle tart in a teashop. There are always people's conversations to be eavesdropped in such places and this can help pass the time. The waitress was very pretty and dressed in traditional black and white and gazing at her fetching figure proved more compulsive than listening to stray conversation.

My next port of call was the public library whose whereabouts I'd already discovered and which I'd found was open until 7.00pm. Here the librarian and his assistants were far from observing "Silence in the Library" and I could not but overhear their chatter. The subject was the state of Devon Library Services, for which organisation I had worked for four years: this was definitely a case of *Plus ça change, plus ça même chose*. I spent a couple of hours contentedly browsing among the shelves. I was rather pleased to find a copy of my own book *Rambles around Newton Abbot* on the shelves. Among the many books I looked at was a reprint of *Old Country Life* by the prolific Devon parson, Sabine Baring Gould. In it he quotes a humorous and entertaining piece of doggerel in which the state of matrimony is compared to a Devonshire lane. This dates, Baring Gould reckons, from the first half of the last century. As I had walked many miles along Devonshire lanes in the past few days I should like to quote the piece here:

In a Devonshire lane, as I trotted along
T'other day, much in want of a subject for song,
Thinks I to myself, I have hit on a strain,
Sure marriage is much like a Devonshire lane.

In the first place 'tis long, and when once you are in it,
It holds you as fast as a cage does a linnet;
For howe'er rough and dirty the road may be found,
Drive forward you must, there is no turning round.

But though 'tis so long, it is not very wide,
For two are the most that together can ride;
And e'en then, 'tis a chance, but they get in a pother,
And jostle and cross and run foul of each other.

Oft poverty greets them with mendicant looks,
And care pushes by them, o'er-laden with crooks;
And strife's grazing wheels try between them to pass,
And stubbornness blocks up the way on her ass.

Then the banks are so high, to the left hand and right,
That they shut out the beauties around them from sight;
And hence you'll allow, 'tis an inference plain,
That marriage is just like a Devonshire lane!

But thinks I too, these banks, within which we are pent,
With bud, blossom, and berry are richly besprent;
And with conjugal fence, which forbids us to roam,
Looks lovely when decked with the comforts of home.

In the rock's gloomy crevice the bright holly grows;
The ivy waves fresh o'er the withering rose,
And the evergreen love of a virtuous wife
Soothes the roughness of care,- cheers the winter of life.

Then long be the journey, and narrow the way,
I'll rejoice that I've seldom a turnpike to pay;
And whate'er others say, be the last to complain,
Though marriage be just like a Devonshire lane.

At seven o'clock the library closed and I began my hunt for a pub for supper. It was then I discovered that there isn't a pub in Tavistock's main street, indeed there are very few pubs at all. The only one that the librarian could remember, though hardly recommend, I found in a back street. The interior resembled an airport lounge of 1950s vintage; the food consisted of a brace of filled rolls staring out from under a plastic lid on the bar counter. The barman could not recommend any other pub where I might get a meal, but did mention a wine bar.

At the wine bar I ate adequately though a little more expensively than usual. The proprietor ackowledged my surprise at the lack of pubs in Tavistock which is the sort of town – attractive, interesting and worth stopping at - where one would expect to find several good hostelries offering food. The much smaller town of Chagford has at least three pubs within a few yards of each other along the main street all offering a good choice of dishes. I took my time over my meal and glass of wine – I'd hung my coat over a chair in front of a convector heater to dry. It was still raining when I returned to the hotel. I watched T.V. in the lounge for a while before retiring to spend the night between those snagged, turquoise, nylon sheets.

Wednesday 23rd May

The next morning at breakfast I met the other guests – two Dutch girls and a Belgian and his English wife. I'd asked the landlady for something other than the usual egg and bacon, and she served up scrambled egg liberally sprinkled with fresh parsley - it was delicious. After advising the Dutch girls on the various parts of Dartmoor worth visiting or avoiding, I packed my rucksack and set out for the day's walking. The rain had stopped and the wind died down; as I had anticipated, the storm had blown itself out. It was overcast and cool but conditions were quite acceptable for the day's activity in hand. I walked along the main road out of Tavistock towards Gunnislake in Cornwall. Thankfully the road has a pavement to the River Lumburn and then it is possible to follow tracks and lanes which take a more direct route to the Tamar. I could see the old mine chimney on the summit of Kit Hill straight ahead.

TON

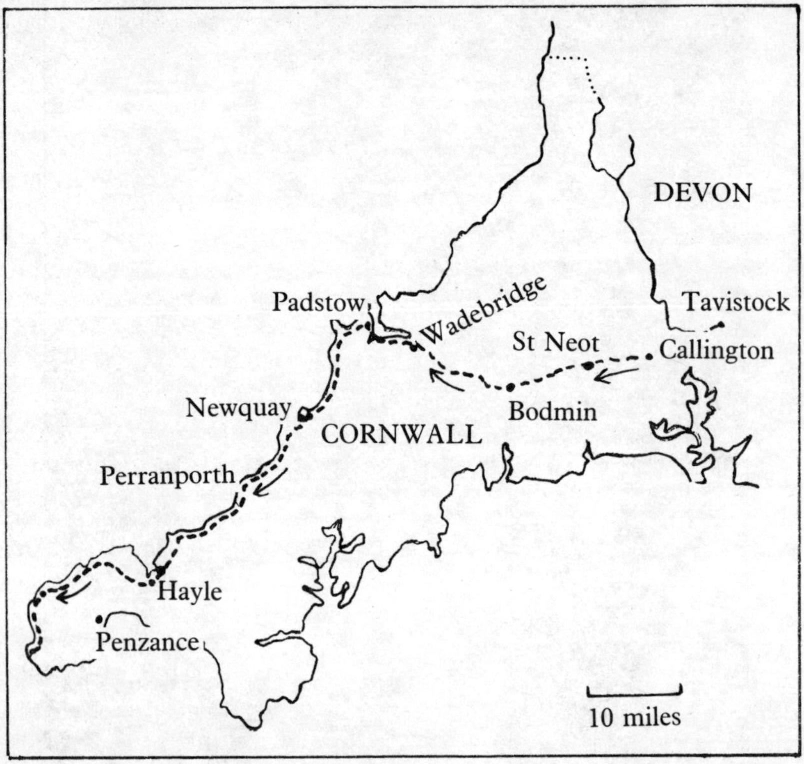

Into Cornwall

8 INTO CORNWALL

I crossed the Tamar and the boundary between Devon and Cornwall. Of all the county boundaries I had encountered on my walk this was by far the most significant. On the far side of the bridge was a signboard with the Cornish coat of arms flanked by a miner and a fisherman, surmounted by a chough and underlined with the Cornish motto *One and All.* I thought about these images, remembering that the chough, a member of the crow family distinguished by its scarlet legs and bill, had been long extinct in Cornwall and was now only to be found on the west coasts of Ireland, Wales, Scotland and the Isle of Man, the rest of the "Celtic fringe". The miner reminded one of the long and enduring story of Cornish metal mining now not nearly as important as it once was. The fisherman still prospers and fishing remains an important industry in the county. The motto *One and All* is no doubt still felt to be true among Cornishmen who retain a great sense of their own identity and separateness from the rest of Britain. Perhaps this was why noticeably fewer people returned my greeting of "Good Morning" as I passed by.

Gunnislake is not the most attractive town in Cornwall and the climb up from the Tamar is long and rather tedious. There are a few shops, a post office and, surprisingly, a railway station; Gunnislake is the terminus of a line up from Plymouth. There is a higher concentration of Bed and Breakfast establishments here than in Devon. I intended to call at a printing works near Callington and left the main road just past the station to take lanes through Albaston and Metherell. These villages are

GRL-G

not neat, nucleated villages like those of Devon and Dorset but rather straggling, with houses stretching away along lanes and dotted about the countryside so that it is difficult to tell where one community ends and another begins. In this respect, this part of East Cornwall reminded me of the far west, the Penwith peninsula, where the villages have a similar character. As in Penwith, here are considerable remains of former mining activity: crumbling chimneys and engine houses and notices warning of mine shafts. Workers' houses were built where the mines were situated and with little regard to existing communities.

Between Albaston and Metherall, where the lane dips into a valley bottom, the road surface was deeply covered with mud. Adjoining the road was a steeply sloping and freshly ploughed field where, as a result of the previous day's downpour, much of the soil had been washed down into the road and had exposed the bare rock beneath.

Looking back I could see the well wooded Tamar Valley, with all the appearance of a gorge in places where crags stood out above the river. Morwhelham was not far away, a hive of activity in the last century, then long abandoned and now being restored under the direction of the Dartington Trust. There is an old copper mine which the visitor can enter on a mine train; the former quay where boats up from Plymouth were loaded with ore from the many mines in the vicinity which produced first copper, then arsenic; the Tavistock Canal from which the copper and arsenic were loaded into trucks which descended on inclined planes to the quay where boats carried the ores down to Plymouth. The head of water from the Tavistock Canal is now employed (since 1933) to turn a water turbine to provide power for the National Grid.

From Metherall I mistakenly took a low road in a valley and saw the printing works, with lights blazing, on the hillside above. There was no right of way across the fields and an old man sawing logs refused to reply to my questions in any way but to answer "No!"

The lane approaching the printing works was lined with cars and a lorry was unloading rolls of paper. As I approached the office there were signs that there had recently been a fire. I was told that they had indeed suffered a conflagration two weeks before – there had been considerable damage to the fabric of the building, to some expensive machinery in the factory, and to the office end which was now hastily being rebuilt. The insurance would cover the cost of the damage but deliveries had got behind and customers were becoming impatient. I had a cup of coffee and spent about an hour talking to someone in the design studio where the typesetting and artwork is carried out.

The road into Callington passes the large Ginsters factory whose vans, which bear the slogan *Pasties fresh from Cornwall daily*, are a familiar sight on West Country roads. In one part of the building I noticed a lot of white coated and hatted workers and, further on, a place open to the public where one could eat no end of pasties and other Ginsters products. I don't very much like pasties or anything in the category of mass-produced meat products but thought my entry into Cornwall should be celebrated with a sample of its most famous dish. The counter faced a vast array of seating although the place was completely empty. The girl serving told me it was takeaway only, which seemed rather curious in the circumstances, so I made that my excuse not to order but to press on into Callington to find somewhere to sit down for a snack.

It was 2.00pm when I walked out of Callington past St Mary's Church. The clouds were clearing and the sun breaking through to spotlight Caradon Hill; the country looked greener and fresher and the air was clear after the previous day's downpour. I headed due west along narrow country lanes and field paths via Haye, Trevigro and Penwarden to an old mill and bridge across the River Lynher. Unfortunately there is no public right of way through Bicton Wood on the far bank and one is forced to take a detour upstream to reach the lane to Pensilva. This is a largish village which stretches for about a mile along the road. The western end of the village – where there is much recent housing – is marked by a cattle grid. Here is the boundary between the enclosed lands of Pensilva and the open, sheep-bitten slopes of Caradon Hill. I continued in a westerly direction under Caradon Hill, crowned by a TV mast and scarred by the detritus of past mining activity. For a while I left the road and followed the track bed of an old railway which runs close by.

At the crossroads at Crow's Nest I headed south-west to Trevethy Quoit. This is marked in Gothic script on the O.S. map thus indicating a non-Roman antiquity which I thought might be worth a visit. On the far side of the valley approaching the ancient monument I could see the pinnacles on the tower of the church at St Cleer. To the south-east Plymouth, to the south at several points the sea and to the west the broken landscape of St Austell. Trevethy Quoit stands close by some houses in a field just off the road and consists of a few massive granite slabs. They are arranged vertically to enclose a space and capped by a single slab. The whole structure would once have been covered with earth which has subsequently eroded away. A plaque explains that this is "a burial chamber probably built and used as a collective tomb" and dates it as "Early Bronze Age 1800-1200 BC". I stood marvelling at the simplicity of its construction and the feat achieved by its makers in transporting and erecting such massive pieces of masonry. I mused too, upon the thought that such men should leave as their most lasting remains a memorial to their dead.

From Trevethy Quoit I followed an enchanting path down to the valley below St Cleer. This old way was evidently some kind of boundary path; it was deep and narrow and flanked by stone and turf walls and arched over by spindly trees. The fields either side were at shoulder level, the bright sun shone through the branches above and produced a flickering effect as I walked along. In addition to the usual array of wild flowers were clumps of bracken, the young delicate fronds springing from the walls seemed like hands reaching out. A light breeze caused the bracken to quiver gently and this movement, together with

Trevethy Quoit, ancient burial chamber

the fugitive sunlight from above and the broken shadows on the ground produced a hypnotic effect as I proceeded downhill. I stopped several times to gather myself and to absorb the magic of this ancient path. I took a photograph and half expected and half wished that the resultant picture would reveal some Cornish pixies dancing along the path (sadly, it did not).
St Cleer is a contrast to Pensilva - it is a compact village with its buildings well gathered about its church, a handsome edifice with a rugged, granite tower, sitting prettily in its tree-lined grounds. From St Cleer I continued in a westerly direction along a little used lane until I reached a steep descent to the River Fowey which flows down from Bodmin Moor. Here are two bridges: the newer, broader one just downstream is the one currently in use as a road bridge; the other is a narrow bridge of obvious antiquity and a notice indicates "Treverbyn Bridge c.1412". I sat on the wall of the old bridge for a while, my eyes straying from the rushing waters of the Fowey to a field beyond in which a tractor was cutting the hay. The sun felt quite strong in this sheltered spot and the air was clearer than it had been for a week or more. It was now approaching evening and I thought I should try to find a place to stay in the next village – St.Neot.

I had considered reaching the legendary Warleggan but thought accommodation there might be rather expensive on account of its *Poldark* connections. As I descended the hill to St.Neot one of the lenses in my spectacles fell out and smashed in the road. I was relieved that I'd remembered to pack a spare pair - I should have been quite literally lost without my specs. St Neot soon came into focus and I saw at a glance that this was the most attractive place I'd seen since Tavistock. The village lies either side of a valley which carries the River Loveny south to meet the Fowey a couple of miles downstream. The most attractive Church of St.Neot commands a dominant position on the west facing hill. Just below the church and of more immediate interest is the London Inn.

A sign indicated "Accommodation" and the name of the hostelry was a persuasive invitation to one walking from that city to Land's End, notwithstanding that bed and breakfast in a pub was likely to be relatively expensive. The landlord told me that The London Inn did not, in fact, provide accommodation and that he must get around to amending the noticeboard; he did, however, give me the names and whereabouts of a couple of places in the village. I was pleased to note that the inn did provide meals. I found my billet for the night – a modern bungalow with a comfortable, old-fashioned double bed and, joy of joys, winceyette sheets. I had a bath which was a sheer delight and afterwards performed the evening foot medication ritual.

It was a beautiful, calm, still and sunlit evening as I walked over to the pub. I was the only customer, a fact that was brought to my attention by the barmaid in a mildly suggestive way. The pub had filled up slightly by the time I left – most eyes looked towards two young men who fed an endless stream of coins into one of those bleeping, flashing, electronic machines that seem to devour money, in order to bleep and flash the more and, from time to time, as if suffering from indigestion, to regurgitate a little of what it has so hastily gobbled up. The machine's two players were convinced they could beat its electronic brain and after the best part of an hour began to fall out with each other as it became clear that the machine had won. Back outside into that cool, serene evening whose fading blue sky now tinged with the fiery glow of the setting sun promised a fine day to follow.

Thursday 24th May

Having breakfasted amply in a room with an inspiring view over the village towards the church I bade my Cornish hosts farewell and climbed up the hill westwards. It felt decidedly warmer under a clear blue sky. Once again the road reached a moory top; the O.S. map shows the unclassified roads as dashed lines in such places and this cartographic device gives a fair impression of the change from fields with boundaries defined by hedges to open, unenclosed common where the road seems subservient to the gorse, bracken and grazing sheep. This is Goonzion Downs which cover only a small area and which I had soon crossed to reach Pantersbridge which spans the River Bedalder, another minor tributary of the Fowey. Pantersbridge is a rerun of Treverbyn Bridge - the modern road bridge is accompanied by the original medieval bridge, this one dated *c*.1415.

The first village I passed through was Mount; here an old man shouted at me from his front garden on the opposite side of the lane, "'Ow far are 'e gonna go, then?" "To Land's End!", I shouted back at him. An audible gasp from the old man prompted me to tell him how far I'd come; this was followed by a louder gasp still and the further question, "And 'ave 'e walked all the way?"

From Mount up once more onto the moor-like tops – here known as Treslea Downs – which are so much a feature of this part of East Cornwall, a kind of sub-Bodmin Moor. The tower of St.Menbred Church at Cardinham soon came into view and I descended to this small hamlet, with its tennis court and rather unCornish appearance. I spent some time attempting to find the right of way from Cardinham to the wooded valley to the south west. In the absence of any signposting I struck out across a field, following the lowest contour to the valley ahead. I soon reached a field boundary with barbed wire and tore my right trouser leg in my attempt to cross it. I eventually found my way down to Milltown at the head of Cardinham Woods.

Granite signpost

These woods, which are under the auspices of the Forestry Commission, extend for over two miles either side of this tributary of the Fowey and the Forest Walks provided are most attractive. I followed the track on the southern bank of the river and the scene from here had an almost alpine character. Tall fir trees predominated on the slopes, whilst in the valley bottom grew silver birch, poplar, beech and ash. The trees are not regimented in straight lines as in many plantations but exhibit a natural, chaotic appearance. It was exceedingly quiet and peaceful in this wooded valley, the only sounds being the rustle of leaves in the intermittent breeze, the swirl of the river when it was close enough to the path to be audible and the occasional crack of a twig underfoot.

I did not see a soul until I reached the end of the wood and spotted a woman beside the stream below the track. She was not looking up so I passed on. A couple of minutes later the calm was shattered by the loud and fierce barking of a dog: I looked back and there was an Alsatian running towards me. I was upwind from the dog and he had evidently caught my scent. The beast circled round me, barking menacingly and all but sinking his jaws into my lower limbs. I soon saw his mistress (the woman I'd seen on the river bank) approaching and I remained where I was until she had caught up with us, taken the dog by the collar and calmed him down. The truth is I don't much like large dogs, Alsatians most particularly; their barking and general hostility quite confounds me. I was planning to tell the dog's owner what I thought of her wild beast but in the event I simply said, "I'm afraid I can't handle those things"; she was very nice about it and said her thing was an eight-month old bitch which was not yet quite civilised. I walked along with her to the forester's house where she lived.

From Cardinham Woods I followed the lane towards Bodmin. The hedgebanks hereabouts were a riot of red campion, stitchwort and bluebells: red, white and blue. A brimstone butterfly added a splash of yellow. Another butterfly caught my eye which I noted as having pale green wings marked by a few brown spots and veined like a leaf. On later checking an identification guide I find that it looks very much like the Cleopatra butterfly which is a South European species occurring in Spain, Italy and North Africa and only very occasionally, and then by accident, in Britain. Females are apparently very similar to those of the brimstone so I suppose what I saw was not a rare accident but a female brimstone. The brimstone was originally known as the "butter-coloured fly" which gave us our word "butterfly".

I crossed the track of the Bodmin Branch Railway line twice and the new dual carriageway A30 Bodmin bypass and walked along the road below Bodmin Castle towards town. There was much new building here, including industrial units; ahead I could see the Beacon and to the south and west a long view into central Cornwall.

Cornish place names have a fascination greater than those in other parts of England; the influence of the old Celtic language once spoken here gives rise to some interesting and, to the non-Cornishman, extremely foreign sounding names. East Cornwall seems less Cornish, at least as far as place names go, than further west and there are many English sounding names mixed in with the more authentically Cornish. As I approached Bodmin I recalled a very amusing little book which had been published about six months before entitled *The Meaning of Liff* (Pan, 1983). This book is an A to Z of selected British place names which suggests new meanings for these attractive but underused words.

Bodmin is defined as follows: "The irrational and inevitable discrepancy between the amount pooled and the amount needed when a large group of people try to pay a bill together after a meal." This prompted a new train of thought which kept me occupied for many moments during my walk through Cornwall. All my definitions seemed to relate to the follies of walking, hence:

> *Redruth* (a town on the A30 further west): medical term referring to the condition where the pads of one's feet become red and sore following the first few days of a long distance walk.
> *Nancledra* (a village northwest of Penzance): medical term referring to the condition of premature ageing characterised by shuffling feet and a faraway look in the eyes, often the fate of those who indulge in a surfeit of walking.
> *Woon Gumpus* (a common near Pendeen in the far west); a term which connotes that feeling of utter contentment, following a long day's walking and a sound night's sleep, when one awakes with wonderfully rested limbs, looks at one's watch and realises that one can luxuriate for a full half hour before rising to enjoy that huge breakfast.

I had never visited Bodmin before, although I had driven by it down the A30 many times. I passed the railway terminus and followed a footpath to Priory Park. This led past a fine house which contains the offices of North Cornwall District Council to reach St Petroc's Church. Bodmin seemed a bright and lively place with more to it than simply shops. I walked through the town and found myself outside the Public Library. The memorial listing the names of dead of the First and Second World Wars had now been inscribed with the names of two killed in the Falklands and one in Northern Ireland. I noticed too, that this was a Passmore Edwards Library and that discovery triggered a flood of memories of my years at Newton Abbot. That library was housed in a building donated by the Cornish philanthropist John Passmore Edwards. Edwards' life was a story of rags to riches and a character at once modest and full of a sense of Christian duty to his fellow humans. Apart from a rather shallow work – a eulogy to the great man – which was published soon after his death, no one has ever written his biography. He had a long life full of endeavour and achievement though apparently without scandal.

Passmore Edwards was born in Blackwater, a small village

between Redruth and Truro, in 1823. His mother, whose maiden name was Passmore, was a native of Newton Abbot – hence his gift of a library to that town, about the only gift he made outside his own Cornwall or his adopted London.

In Newton Abbot Library there stood on a window sill on the staircase a bust of the library's benefactor cast in red Watcombe clay. He looks like a cross between Karl Marx and Father Christmas with his bushy beard and kindly, patriarchal air. I developed a real affection for the old man, our founder, whose name lived on in the moulding above the entrance: "This Building was Presented to the Town by J. Passmore Edwards in Memory of his Mother" and another nearby which commemorated his visit in 1902 to lay the foundation stone.

I intended to call on a publisher in Padstow later that day and realised I would not reach that place until very late in the afternoon if I was to walk all the way. I stepped out of Bodmin on the main road to Wadebridge and, as I descended the hill to the River Camel I began halfheartedly to thumb a ride. It was still a splendid day and the partly wooded Camel valley below looked very inviting. As I really wanted to walk I gave up the idea of hitch-hiking after a few minutes and descended by field path to Nanstallon. The walk along the lane beyond this place did not disappoint – here were woods and fields sloping down to the River Camel. The pylons and crackling overhead cables swooping across the valley did not add to the attractions of the scene. It seems a rule in Cornwall that whenever one comes downhill one meets a river or stream before one ascends once again. I suppose this would seem blindingly obvious to a native but to one more familiar with the dry combes of the chalk downs the presence of a babbling brook in every hollow in the hills is a refreshing and welcome sight.

I was surprised to see some light aircraft in a field in a tributary valley below Ruthernbridge. A comparatively steep and narrow valley seemed an odd place for an airfield. I now entered a Forestry Commission track which led me through a wood above the river. I emerged from the wood and climbed up to Burlawn where a most attractive track led down to Treaven, just above Wadebridge. At the farm I wasn't sure of the way ahead and the farmer asked me if I'd lost myself, which seemed a much more graphic expression than asking whether I was lost. He put me right and I followed a field path at the edge of a corn field which sloped down to Wadebridge. Beyond were the 17 arches of the medieval bridge at the head of the Camel estuary and Egloshayle, the community on the east bank.

As I descended to meet the river I noticed that it had stopped flowing which I guessed indicated that it was high tide. On the far side of town I found the track of the old Padstow branch line railway, marked on the O.S. map as the Wadebridge-Padstow Path, which I intended to follow. A notice at the start of the path declares, "This path is for use by walkers, pedal cyclists and horse riders. Please give priority to walkers", which seems the correct priority. However, the start of the path is metalled and my first companion was a Volvo which whizzed past down river, then an enormous digger which was grumbling along towards me in the opposite direction. Next came half a dozen young lads on their BMX bikes. I spotted a curiosity in the shape of a "fence" between fields built of large, upended stone slabs. This, unfortunately, was in a poor state of repair with many gaps and much fallen masonry. The metalled road gave way to railway chippings at a point where a new sewage works was under construction; I was comforted with the thought that a bit less human manure would be finding its way into the sea.

After a mile or two the breeze grew stronger and cooler as it blew in from the ocean up the widening estuary. Then conditions changed dramatically. What had been a warm, clear, sunny day now became cool, murky and overcast. The sun was blotted out in a grey haze. At first I could see across the estuary to the whalebacked Cant Hill but within a few minutes visibility was reduced to about 100 yards; I could not see anything of Padstow when I crossed the old girder bridge which carried the railway across a creek just south of the town. The white sea mist was being swept inland by the on-shore wind and could be seen billowing up the sloping fields. As a result the beauties of the Camel estuary, which I had not visited before, all but vanished. Visual detail was confined to the path itself, along the sides of which I noticed red valerian and dog daisies, the first I'd seen on my walk. With your sense of sight impaired, your sense of hearing becomes magnified, or is it a trick of the sea mist to enlarge otherwise distant sounds? I could hear a persistent cuckoo which sounded very close but must have been calling from the far side of the estuary.

I reached Padstow, first beside the ubiquitous modern bungalows, then by Victorian villas; finally I found the old heart of the town. I was almost startled to see people here. The peculiar effects of the all-enveloping mist unconsciously led me to expect Padstow to be devoid of human life, to be a ghost town. I followed my nose downhill until I reached the sea. It was the fishing boats that seemed out of place in a harbour which is surrounded by shops selling nothing but merchandise aimed at the tourist, an apparently vanishing species. I had intended to regain the coast-path at Padstow; from here I planned to follow the North Cornwall Coast Path to the Far West. There was a Youth Hostel at Treyarnon Bay, about 5 miles west of Padstow, and another at Perranporth, about one third of the way to Land's End.

I'd had some correspondence with a publisher in Padstow in recent months and in my last letter had said I'd call and see her on my way through. It was early evening when I knocked at her door: I was concerned that this would be an inconvenient time and I was concious of my somewhat unkempt appearance, torn trousers and all. The umbrella I'd bought in Tavistock perhaps lent me an air of respectability (or did it just look rather eccentric?), but publishers were surely not people to stand on ceremony.

I left my rucksack and brolly in the hall and was shown into a large, book-lined drawing room. A tray of rather superior tasting tea and cake was produced. I squeezed out several cups and spent an enjoyable hour talking with this independent publisher who has a most interesting and diverse list of titles including a number of literary biographies and memoirs of general as well as Cornish interest. When I emerged I was tempted to find a bed and breakfast in Padstow but soon decided to press on to Treyarnon Bay though I abandoned the coast path and its circuitous route via Trevose Head to follow the B-road via Treator and St.Merryn and thence by lane and fieldpath. About half way to Treyarnon the mist suddenly cleared and the sun appeared as a glowing, red ball which felt warm in the still evening air.

The Youth Hostel at Treyarnon is housed in a large house close to the beach and I found it after walking through a camping and caravan site and turning right at some public conveniences. It was almost dark when I reached it; I'd been on the road approaching 12 hours with only an hour's break in Padstow. I'd grabbed a pretty ghastly bag full of fish and chips at St.Merryn and now bought a Mars bar from the hostel shop. I felt too exhausted even to walk out and view the Atlantic Ocean.

After checking in for bed and breakfast and bathing my feet I sat down with an old copy of *Cycling Times* and read an article in which the Chairman of the Youth Hostels Association was interviewed about the present state and future of the organisation. Membership had peaked in 1980 – that was the YHA Jubilee Year and the attendant publicity had resulted in a boost in membership; three years later membership was down by 17%, a number of hostels had closed and many more were being used far short of capacity. The YHA had not, apparently, been moving with the times, but soon would be. Did this mean video games and mixed dormitories? Video games – yes, in some hostels. Mixed dormitories - over the Chairman's dead body, although these had been introduced in France. The cost of a night in a Youth Hostel was surely now more, in real terms, than 20 years ago when I was an active hosteller. Perhaps that had something to do with it. The YHA seemed to be in a similar position to many other businesses - it was being forced to push up prices and curtail services which led to an inexorable decline. The hostels at Tavistock and Hayle had closed in recent years, although both are indicated by red triangles on the relevant O.S. maps. Probably mass unemployment among young people has as much to do with the decline in the use of hostels as anything.

I was the only person out of the half dozen or so staying at the hostel – a decidedly mature collection of individuals – who asked for breakfast, as the warden informed me. I offered to forgo breakfast, wanting to avoid any inconvenience to my host, but my offer was turned down. I retired to the dormitory where the only other occupant was a New Zealander on a motorcycle (the latter he left outside the building). I read a few pages of an old book, *The Delectable West*, which I'd found under the *Cycling Times* but was too exhausted to take in anything.

Friday 25th May

My room mate arose at the ungodly hour of 6.15am – perhaps he didn't have many days in which to see Britain. When he returned from the lavatory he urged me to get up. I certainly wasn't getting up at 6.30 and carried on studying my O.S. map to survey the coming day's walk. At 6.45 the warden came in to tell me my breakfast had been ready for 15 minutes. Why was everybody about so early? Perhaps Treyarnon Bay was a special early rising hostel.

Breakfast consisted of two fried eggs, four sausages and a slurry of baked beans, accompanied by cornflakes, a pot of tea, toast and marmalade. Had the warden taken his revenge for the inconvenience of providing a solitary breakfast by giving me so much to get through? No, he was surely simply being generous. I just about managed to work my way through, washed my crockery and returned it to the warden. Everyone else had gone and I asked if he wanted me to perform a duty. He said he'd prefer it if I'd just leave. This sounded decidedly unfriendly and I made some remark about the fact that he ran an extremely early rising hostel. He countered by pointing out that it was 9.40. But my watch said it was 8.10! It was then I realised my watch was one and a half hours slow; I apologised for my tardiness and left as soon as I could – this was the latest start of my three week walk.

The sky was overcast, though it was fairly bright, and there was a moderate northerly wind blowing as I crossed Treyarnon Beach to reach the headland opposite. The cliffs here are not particularly high but they are indeed spectacular. From Treyarnon to Porthcothan the west-facing coast is deeply indented and the path follows headland and cove in rapid succession. At first sight of the rocks and the sea I was transfixed. There were long trails of foam between the coast and the outlying stacks. The contrast with West Dorset and East Devon was striking - there the sea had been calm as glass under an inert, hazy sky, the undulating hills ending at the shore and facing the sea as crumbling, near horizontal, sedimentary strata. Here the sea was continually heaving and boiling about the jagged slaty rocks. Land and sea were fully engaged in the struggle for supremacy. This, of course, was no mere channel between continent and offshore island, but the Atlantic Ocean.

"From Treyarnon to Porthcothan the west-facing coast is deeply indented"

The coast path to Porthcothan and beyond is a relatively easy walk – a good deal less up and down than I had experienced during the two previous days through East Cornwall. Central Cornwall is more of a plateau than the crinkled landscape further east. Although one is here completely exposed to the elements, the path itself is a smooth carpet of green turf rolled out along the cliff top from which my field of vision included the rocks, beaches and the sea, the view ahead towards Newquay and beyond, inland towards fields bounded by stone and turf walls. At one's feet, bristling in the wind, were pillows of sea pinks, yellow kidney vetch and, in more sheltered spots, white sea campion. Herring gulls perched on the cliff edge beside the path waiting until the last possible moment before alighting at my approach. The slaty rock is shiny silver grey where washed by the sea, especially where it forms flat ledges over which the water runs back and forth; it is blacker where exposed to the sky.

The stone and turf walls here and throughout Cornwall are objects of some interest, as are the stiles which give passage through them. The walls are built in layers of slaty rock stacked herring-bone fashion, leaning first one way, then the other, like badly kept bookshelves. The tops are sometimes finished off with a vertically stacked layer but usually with turf from which all manner of wild flowers are seen to grow, and even trees. The roots are able to penetrate the oblique layers of stone and the result is to strengthen the wall by binding together its various sections, rather than to weaken it. At ends and corners larger stones tend to be employed and are laid horizontally in order to give these more vulnerable parts greater stability. Stiles are invariably stone rather than wood and most often consist of large pieces of masonry arranged to form one or more steps up to a central stone over which one must manoeuvre to reach the steps down on the other side. A common arrangement is to employ long rectangular blocks of solid granite built into the wall either side. In this case the stile need not be a solid structure but sufficient obstacle to cattle and aid to pedestrians. This pattern varies in the far west of Cornwall, as we shall see. I reached the cliff above Bedruthan Steps, a distinctive and awe-inspiring stretch of the North Cornwall Coast Path, and passed close to a National Trust shop and car park - an oasis of commerce. It seems odd that the National Trust, of all people, should want to open a shop selling such trivia as herb-scented soap and commemorative mugs in such an otherwise unspoilt spot.

Hereabouts I noticed the appearance of a flower I had not

seen before: a lowly blue flower with six-pointed petals like a star - this was the spring squill. About a mile beyond the National Trust bazaar I passed a bench seat which bore an *In Memoriam* plaque and was constructed from four smoothly cut rectangles of granite: two legs, a seat and a backrest. Rounding Trenance Point, the wide, flat, sandy inlet below the village suddenly opened up. The whole place was deserted, except for a couple of coastguards moving their red and yellow flags up the beach as the tide rushed in, all for the benefit of non-existent swimmers.

It was about lunchtime when I called at a beach-side café, also totally deserted, and indulged in a piece of cherry pie and cream. I felt guilty about the cream as I always do, but justified my greed on the grounds that the effort of the next few miles would be bound to break down all that cholesterol. I would have declined the cream on grounds of expense, if not health, had I known that the dollop of Real Cornish Clotted Cream cost an extra 35p. As I climbed out of Trenance towards Berryl's Point rain began to fall. I pulled on my waterproof trousers; the wind was a constant north/north-easterly blast which conveniently jammed my brolly down over my head, shoulders and rucksack. Just as I began to feel nicely protected from the elements, the rain ceased.

I followed the coast path above Watergate Bay and the great sprawl of Newquay – the nearest Cornwall has to a Brighton or a Blackpool - grew closer. Newquay has everything that English seaside resorts are famous for, including amusement arcades, endless souvenir shops, candy floss, sticks of rock and much more. It was the Friday before Spring Bank Holiday. The damp grey weather indicated this if not the dearth of visitors. It really must be a fact that Bank Holiday weekends tend to be cold and wet; it would be almost disappointing it they were not so. I thought back to August Bank Holiday in 1976, the Year of the Great Drought and the Incredibly Hot Summer. My family and I were lying on a beach in South Devon on the Monday afternoon when the sky clouded over and the first drops of rain to fall for several months descended upon the bronzed bodies of sunbathers. Quite spontaneously a cheer arose from the parched masses, delighted that it should have begun raining, and on August Bank Holiday Monday of all days!

To be fair to Newquay, the resort has a sophistication that other Cornish resorts cannot emulate. Bed and Breakfast establishments, guest houses and hotels are thick on the ground and their noticeboards proclaim their respective attributes to the comfort-loving and diversion-seeking punters. Here you may enjoy not only colour TV, central heating, en suite rooms (your own personal loo), licensed bars and games rooms with pool tables, but heated indoor and outdoor swimming pools, squash courts, saunas and solariums too. Surely more like Majorca than Newquay, apart from the central heating.

I still had several miles to make before reaching Perranporth where I planned to spend the night at the Youth Hostel; Newquay certainly did not invite me to linger. My immediate target was the deep inlet south of Newquay known as The Gannel, where the O.S. map showed both a ferry crossing and a footpath. I found my way down to the shore where the high tide had all but flooded the inlet. I got my bearings but could see no sign of a ferry nor any evidence of a right of way across the water, except for a public footpath sign indicating the continuation of the route on the opposite shore. I made my way "downstream" in the direction of the ferry but was stopped at a point where the sandy shore meets rocky cliffs, with no right of way above but only private gardens. Neither could I see any evidence that a ferry was actually in operation. I approached two middle-aged ladies whom I assumed must be locals; just as I asked them about crossing the Gannel they asked me the same question. They were neither locals nor much help. The detour inland around the head of this inlet would add 4 or 5 miles to my walk but I could see no option.

As I headed back "upstream" and passed the supposed crossing point I spotted, a couple of feet beneath the surface of the clear water, a plank bridge. So this was the crossing! The tide was ebbing rapidly and I decided to wait until I could cross. It began to rain and I sat down on a rock under my umbrella and waited for the moon to do her work of drawing the water. As its level fell I could see that the bridge did not actually reach the opposite shore – it seemed to end in midstream. As I waited the bridge surfaced on my side but seemed to dip down under the water before reaching its premature end. I decided to take off my boots and socks and investigate. I reached the end of this eccentric bridge and tested the depth with my brolly – it was no more than knee deep. Clutching boots, socks and umbrella I took the plunge and waded my way to the sand on the far shore. There I met a party of ramblers coming towards me whom I was able to advise. There seemed little point in having a bridge which was only half a bridge and which was submerged half the time, though perhaps a complete bridge which gave access to the far side all the time would be too easy. A reasonable compromise would be a notice informing the inexperienced pedestrian that, at high tide, half a bridge was temporarily hidden from view.

I reached Crantock after first losing my way and phoned the youth hostel at Perranporth to check there was room – there was plenty. From Crantock I crossed Cubert Common and an area of sand dunes to reach Penhale Camp which I mistakenly expected to be a holiday camp. It turned out to be an army camp: at the main gate I found a large notice saying "Unauthorised Persons Prohibited". I supposed I was an Unauthorised Person although I didn't really feel I was such. I'd planned to cut through Penhale Camp to Perran Bay to follow the coastal footpath directly to Perranporth.

Behind the beach is a large area of sand dunes, the north part of which is used by the army as a training area while the south part is occupied by holiday camps. There are no convenient rights of way for the coastal walker, or so I concluded, so there was nothing for it but to take a detour inland via Ellenglaze and Mount. From Holywell a footpath formed a boundary between

Penhale sand dunes and a caravan site in which the rows of identical vans were all painted off-white with off-green trimmings and orange curtains. The area teemed with rabbits which constantly criss-crossed the path ahead of me; from the direction of Penhale Camp came the sound of a bugle. There was a thatched roof at Ellenglaze - one of only two I was to see in Cornwall – and beyond this hamlet an area of boggy ground with yellow flags and marsh marigolds which the footpath crossed with the aid of several little bridges made of railway sleepers. Beyond the bog came a sandy field carpeted with cowslips. The minor road to the south west of Mount was bordered with white bluebells and white campion; just beyond the point at which it meets the road linking Perranporth to the A30 I followed a right of way across a golf course where notices warn the walker to "Beware of Golfers". A stream flows out onto the beach at Perranporth; now the sky was dramatic with broken cloud and sun sinking in the west. It was getting late and I was anxious to reach the hostel but had to find a meal first.

As I entered the town I approached a large pub whose appearance did not attract me but the menu chalked up on blackboards outside did. It was one of those pubs where you feel decidedly out of place for being on the wrong side of 20. I asked for a pint of draught Guinness and, as this was being pulled, for the menu. The barmaid told me there was no food being served so I asked her to leave the draught Guinness at half a pint and I would go elsewhere. There wasn't elsewhere – the only takeaways were fish and chip shops and a dubious looking Chinese. There was a wine bar however. Here was a choice of spaghetti, chili, moussaka and something else which were all about the same price and inexpensive. I chose the moussaka and a glass of house red. The wine was pulled up by handpump and really was very poor: thin and vinegary. The moussaka was a joke – a few lumps of very old potato hiding a fragment of tomatoey meat with a hint of cheese melted on top – a total absence of aubergine or any kind of flavouring. There was every sign that other diners were actually enjoying their meals. I left as soon as I could, without complaint, and found the coastal path around Droskyn Point to the Youth Hostel.

Perranporth Hostel is graded as Simple: it is a single storey building of rather make-shift appearance on the seaward side of the footpath around a rocky headland. The setting is spectacular: the headland slopes down to the path and then drops much more precipitously seaward. The view from the hostel takes in the wide sweep of Perran Beach towards Ligger and Penhale Points, the cliffs south-west towards St Agnes and far out across the ocean. I met the warden, checked in, bought a packet of biscuits and met the one other guest. Having treated my feet, I emerged from the dormitory to find warden and guest engrossed in a game of Scrabble. The sun was setting over the sea – a flaming red point on the horizon highlighting the clouds and the ocean. I rushed out to take a photograph.

Back in the common room I browsed through a couple of old railway magazines but, feeling I simply had to get myself into a horizontal position, made my excuses and went to bed. I had made up my bed in the lower bunk under the window. This was a mistake. The metal window frame was so badly corroded that it would not shut and there was a fearful draught. I dropped off very quickly, however, but awoke in the middle of the night. The wind had increased and I lay there enjoying the incessant buffetting sounds it created. I felt I was on a vessel at sea – the imagined rocking boat soon coaxed me back to sleep.

Saturday 26 May

The warden turned out to be a bit of a philosopher and I enjoyed a chat with him over breakfast. He was concerned at the declining popularity of youth hostels but felt they should not change in a bid to reverse the trend. Youth hostels appealed to a minority of the population and it was no good pretending otherwise – there were already too many people using hostels purely for convenience and not entering into the spirit of the thing.

I bade my host farewell, stepped out of the hostel onto the coast path and turned right. There is a gap in the coverage of the North Cornwall Coast Path between the two 1:50,000 O.S. maps (Nos 200 and 203). I guessed I should be able to follow the coast path to the far side of St.Agnes where Sheet 203 can be referred to. There was a very strong northerly wind and the sea was much more broken and flecked with foam than the on previous day. The cliff path is no more than a narrow track clinging to this steep, rocky slope above the sea; the vegetation predominantly heather and, surprisingly, primroses. The coast here is scarred with old workings for tin: there are many former mine shafts which have been capped with a cone-shaped framework of steel. I tossed stones into one or two to see how far they would fall.

The path becomes indistinct amid this confusion of spoil heaps, shafts and excavations and I found myself crossing an airfield. There were runways in good repair and a windsock but no sign whatever of any aircraft. I crossed the airfield, rather nervously, and thought of an incident in my aircraft spotting youth. A friend and I were at Stansted Airport, it was sometime towards the end of the 1950s and this airport was very much in the doldrums - I think we only saw one aircraft land all day. Through our binoculars we spotted, at the far side, between a couple of hangars, what we thought was an old Brabazon. We crept around the edge of the airfield towards our quarry, then crossed a runway on our way back to the public area. Half way across the tarmac a yellow Civil Airports Authority Land Rover came screaming towards us at full speed with emergency bells ringing. We got a severe ticking off from the driver and his crew – we had shown up as a couple of blips on the radar screen in the control tower and had caused some consternation. Our captors soon calmed down and were being quite kind when we reached the control centre.

Just before reaching St.Agnes, one must descend into Trevellas Porth, where a steep narrow valley, Trevellas Coombe, is an unofficial monument to Cornwall's great mining days; the valley is all but obscured beneath the ruined engine houses, chimneys and heaps of waste. I scrambled across rocks to reach Trevaunance Cove - St Agnes is a little to the south but St Agnes Beacon looms up on the far side of the cove. As I climbed up to the cliff top from St Agnes the wind became a gale but fortunately it was a constant blast from the north-east which pushed one landward rather than seaward. The wind was so strong that the mere act of walking the next couple of miles demanded my full attention. The moment I passed the Coastguard look out on St Agnes Head and turned south the blast quite suddenly ceased: St Agnes Beacon and the cliffs to the north protected the west-facing cliffs from here to Porthtowan.

At Porthtowan notices warn the walker to keep to the public footpath to avoid the danger of subsiding cliffs. Now the coast path follows a narrow passage between the cliff edge and a chain link fence surrounding the M.O.D. property at Nancekuke Common. Much of this fence had collapsed and I wondered if Mr.Heseltine was aware of this shortcoming in our defences. I remembered the name Nancekuke from a time, many years ago, when I was hitch-hiking around Cornwall and I had a ride with a friendly lorry driver. As we passed Nancekuke Common he pointed out a field of crops which had withered, looked quite dead and made a strange picture on that summer's day. "Them military fellows been and poisoned them crops", he told me, adding, "I can't understand why they should go and ruin a good

Mine engine house near St.Agnes

field o' potatoes like that, it's criminal." The military fellows had evidently been testing defoliant chemicals. At the end of the fenced area were some Kafkaesque looking concrete slab buildings, apparently without doors or windows. I passed a lone walker before the descent to Portreath.

On the far side of Portreath the coast path traversed the Carvamel and Reskajeage Downs, owned by the National Trust. The walking became more like the smooth green strip of carpet that I'd found the day before as I left Treyarnon Bay. The B3301 from Portreath to Hayle touches the coast path at a point about half way between Portreath and Godrevy Point. As I walked by the inevitable car park a little notice at my feet, just between the path and the cliff edge, seemed from the corner of my eye to read "No Jumping". Surely not! Anyone contemplating suicide would be bound to disobey such an order in a negative and depressed frame of mind. I turned back to check it out. "No Dumping" was the message. However, the amount of garbage clinging to the craggy cliff indicated that the order was being regularly ignored.

Beyond Hudder Down the road once again touches the path around Navax and Godrevy Point (I'd had Godrevy lighthouse in full view for the past hour or so) to follow the B-road to the village of Gwithian. Before reaching Gwithian the road led me over the Red River, so aptly named. Red River is a fast-flowing stream of totally opaque, rust-red water. Gwithian has a picturesqueness unusual for an inland Cornish village. I paid a visit to the parish church and was interested to notice a little thatched Methodist Chapel, dated 1810, tucked away nearby. I would have liked to stay in Gwithian and to attend the morning service the next day at the chapel to savour a taste of authentic Cornish Methodism. This was an impractical idea – I had one day left to reach Land's End and felt I had to get as far as Hayle on this, the penultimate day of my journey.

A little further along I left the road and diverged through a car park and across the sand dunes, or towans, towards the sea. The beach was deserted save for a solitary curlew, with its characteristic downward curving beak, which I was pleased to see. The tide was on the ebb but the sea was still vigorous. As each wave stopped its surge forward, the decaying foam left a deposit of red scum on the sand – this was the sediment from the Red River come to a temporary rest. I reached a lifeguard hut and climbed some steps up through a sprawling network of chalets and caravans which eventually led me to the church at Phillack and a view across the inlet to Copperhouse and Hayle.

The wall enclosing the churchyard at Phillack is constructed from large, roughly hewn blocks of black slag and immediately puts one in mind of those soot blackened Victorian churches of industrial towns in the North of England. I crossed the head of the inlet to Copperhouse and turned right along the A30. It must be admitted that, together with Gunnislake, Hayle is not the most inspiring of Cornish towns, although its setting, amid sand dunes, green hills and the flooded valley of the River Hayle should give it a head start. It took me some time to find accommodation. I tried one or two addresses from the RA Bed and Breakfast Guide but they were either full or impossible to locate. I began to walk out of Hayle in the direction of St.Erth and asked in a pub. I was directed to a large comfortable house and was offered excellent accommodation at the most reasonable price thus far: £5.00, and a free pot of tea on arrival.

I later walked about two miles to a pub at the head of the Hayle Estuary which was recommended by my landlady. It was large but chock full of tourists frantically eating and drinking. There was a wide choice of food available and much of it on display and very tempting. The day's "special" was local crab salad and very reasonably priced. I sat down with a pint of Guinness and did not have to wait long for my number to be called. I helped myself to salad, including a generous dollop of almost everything available. The party on my table departed but was soon replaced by a handsome middle-aged couple with whom I soon struck up a conversation. He was a retired international airline pilot and she sold replacement windows. The husband had taken very early retirement and his wife was now the breadwinner. He was happy to potter about on their country estate in a remote valley above Mounts Bay (butterflies were a particular interest). When they learned that I'd walked from London and that the next day was my last they insisted on buying me a drink. We had an enjoyable conversation about Cornwall and some fascinating gossip about the local literary scene.

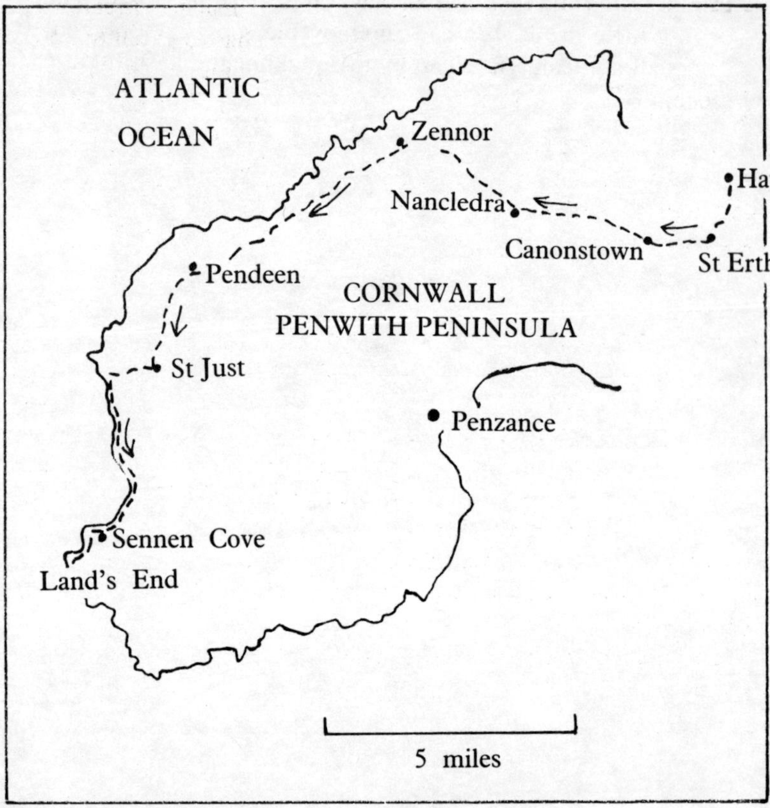

Over the Far West

9 OVER THE FAR WEST

Sunday 27 May

It was Spring Bank Holiday Sunday and a splendid day for walking: bright and sunny, perfect visibility, neither too hot nor too cool, a gentle breeze .... my spirit danced as I set out from Hayle to St Erth, downhill to cross the Hayle River and an imaginary border into West Cornwall or Penwith peninsula. In fact Penwith, the big toe of Cornwall, has a coastline of around 36 miles and is only connected to the rest of the county by a thin, low-lying strip of ground linking St.Ives Bay and Mounts Bay. I crossed the main-line railway to reach the A30 at Canonstown. From here I found an unmade track, then a bridleway which led in the direction of Nancledra. This track was an absolute delight: for half a mile it led past houses, climbing steadily, but then reverted into a narrow but clearly routed boundary path between fields, a designated bridleway. Still climbing, the way is adorned with a profusion of wild flowers and by fields beyond the stone walls. On the north side, below the rock-strewn Trencrom Hill, lies a sharply incised valley which carries a tributary of the Hayle River.

After a couple of miles thus I reached a lane and the village of Nancledra. From here I followed the lane towards Amalveor Downs. Beside the road was a stream and the damp ground gave sustenance to a riot of wild flowers, which only grew less as I gained altitude until the gorse and bracken and a few bluebells predominated. The O.S. map shows no shortage of tracks across the downs of Penwith but far fewer public rights of way. I turned off the lane and across the downs below Trendune Hill via Zennor Quoit to Zennor. None of the tracks here are rights of way but they are fairly well beaten, and being elevated afford some spectacular views south-east across Mounts Bay to the Lizard, north-east along the North Cornish coast dominated by St Agnes' Beacon and north-west and south to the open sea. The ground was peaty and damp and the path I followed was reminiscent of Dartmoor but the proximity and ubiquity of the sea and the indefinable strangeness of West Cornwall made it quite special. Beside the gorse, there were the tiny blue flowers of spring squill and localised outcrops of cotton grass which I left the path to see more clearly.

I recognised the nearby pile of stones as Zennor Quoit only because their appearance resembled the pile at Trevethy Quoit in East Cornwall. As I headed towards the extraordinary outcrop of rocks between Zennor Quoit and the village of that name I met an unlikely looking figure in black leather. He'd just driven down from London and seemed rather overwhelmed by the scene he found now he'd escaped from his car. These rocks are fantastic and almost indescribable. They are composed of granite and exhibit a form of weathering which gives the appearance that they are shedding layers of skin, rather like the layers of an onion. I was drawn to these rocks and simply clambered over and around them taking in the various shapes and masses. I scrambled down the hillside to meet the B3306 St Ives – St Just road.

I'd wanted to visit Zennor because I thought I might just bump into Gerald Priestland, the former broadcaster who lives here and has written a book, West of Hayle River, about Penwith which I much admire. It was now lunch time; church services were over although the church remained open for the benefit of curious visitors. The pub was full. Perhaps G.P. was in the pub; he'd revealed an unexpected penchant for pubs and pints when interviewed on a recent edition of *Desert Island Discs*. But I was not prepared to break my rule about drinking

"The extraordinary outcrop of rocks between Zennor Quoit and the village of that name"

at lunch time so pressed on, leaving G.P. to his Sunday roast, nut rissoles, or whatever.

On past Zennor Museum I rejoined the main road but only briefly. The road is very winding but field paths afford much more direct and pleasanter routes between these meanderings. The field pattern in West Cornwall is distinctive - the fields are tiny and irregular and separated from one another by dry stone walls pierced by stone stiles. Most of these ancient Celtic fields provide pasture for small dairy farms; a few have been left to the gorse and bracken.

The stiles in Penwith are different from their cousins further east. They are really just cattle grids, the iron rails replaced here by slabs of granite and the earth dug out below in order to deter the hooves of straying cattle. A friend has told me that sheep, so often maligned for their lack of intelligence, have devised a method for traversing the more conventional cattle grids which are often found guarding the outskirts of villages in East Cornwall. Here they have learned to perform a commando roll to avoid their legs getting caught in the gaps. Once across they have been found raiding village gardens.

The walls, too, are different. They are composed of granite, but granite which has been picked up from the fields, so that it has been weathered and somewhat rounded. Mortar is not used and nor, for the most part, is the technique of placing turf on top of the stone wall. The walls thus have a character of their own, are rather rough in appearance and, it must be said, none too stable. The light shows through the gaps and, when the sun is directly behind, one catches sight of the most amazing fretwork effect. The fact that light shines through the gaps is intended to deter sheep from attempting to climb the walls.

On the road about half a mile before the Gurnard's Head Hotel I caught sight of a storm out to sea. I saw a black cloud, isolated in an otherwise blue sky with a grey area of rain below it which blotted out the horizon. One could almost see the storm approaching and I wondered if I could reach the Hotel before it struck the coast. I did not quite make it but found myself giving voice to "Singing in the Rain" though not, I confess, skipping down the road Fred Astaire fashion; rather I crouched at the roadside with my brolly jammed down. In fact the rain veered off west and I only caught a little of it. I passed the Gurnard's Head Hotel and remembered visiting it some 19 years previously when I lodged at Pendeen.

I kept to field paths for a mile or two and reached the road again near Morvah. I preferred to walk the road here rather than the Coast Path because I wanted to revisit old haunts. Morvah is no more than a hamlet but has both church and chapel (Wesley A.D.1866). A noticeboard just past the houses indicated the Radjel Inn 1 mile; as it was by now three minutes before two I realised I would not make it before closing time. The road ahead became increasingly familiar, particularly when I reached the crossroads at Higher Boscaswell. The turning left led to Penzance; I had lodged in a cottage just past the crossroads towards Pendeen. I was pleased to see the cottage still in the same place and looking quite unchanged.

Living there had been an experience. The old house had a ground floor of granite slabs while upstairs the rooms were divided by plank walls. My landlady was kind enough but would have won few medals for her generosity. I was ticked off for reading with the light on unless the sun had well and truly sunk over the Atlantic. Beside the landlady and myself the house was inhabited by a yappy little dog whose saving grace for me was as handy dustbin for the unappetising meat which was served with the evening meal. Fortunately my landlady did not eat with me and I was able to slip the unwanted viands under the table.

I had already spent a fortnight in Camborne, sitting my entrance exams to the Camborne School of Mines and getting a taste of work underground in the experimental mine in a granite hill outside the town used by Holman's, the Camborne-based manufacturer of mining equipment. There I was introduced to the rigours of work underground. On the first day we were led to a rock face and set to drilling holes in the solid granite. Everyone knows what a noise pneumatic drills make when they are used to dig up roads. The same drills are used in mines – the noise in a confined space underground is more than twice as loud. It is not simply the rock surface which is drilled, as it is with the hard surface layer of roads, but holes up to six feet deep are worked in order that explosives may be rammed into them.

To start a hole is not easy: the granite resists all attempts at penetration. On that first day I was told to grip the drill steel and keep it at one point on the rock surface until it made some impression and a hole was started. Compressed air is used to power the drill – rubber hoses are trailed along the tunnels from the surface to the face. Water is also pumped through the business end of the drill steel in order to dissolve the large amount of rock dust which is created during the process of drilling. Gripping the drill steel for the first time is rather frightening – the noise, the exhaust from the drill, the jets of water and the almost uncontrollable movement of the drill itself seem overwhelming.

The majority of the young men training at Holman's were from Southern Africa and already had considerable experience of working underground. A minority were black Africans and Asians and I soon discovered that there existed a kind of unofficial but nevertheless very real apartheid between the whites and non-whites. The whites, several of whom had worked in the Rhodesian copper belt, revelled in stories of how many blacks had died in mine accidents and, worst of all, how men were killed when a drill steel snapped and bounced out of the rockface to stab the drill operator, apparently a regular occurrence. Perhaps I took such stories too seriously, and perhaps they were exaggerated to impress me.

My time later in the year at Geevor, one of the few remaining commercially run tin mines in Cornwall, was a different kind of experience. As far as I can remember, I was the only "student" there at the time and I wasn't really given any special treatment except insofar as I had the chance of working in all kinds of situations rather than sticking at one task. I arrived at the mine office as arranged at 9.00am on the first morning and was told by the ill-tempered manager to go home and report back at 7.00am the next morning. The men were out on strike over the employment of a new man who refused to join the union on the grounds of his being a member of the Plymouth Brethren. The next seven weeks were spent working underground on the various manual jobs involved in removing the ore from the narrow "stopes" of metalliferous material which occur in near vertical sheets and cut through the granite bedrock.

At the beginning of a shift I would descend in the usually overloaded cage, equipped with helmet, light and battery to one particular level (there were working levels every 100 feet down to about 1500 feet) where I would be assigned to a miner for the day. My first job was at the 900 feet level: trucks would be emptied at certain points where the ore was dumped onto a grill before descending to a lower level. Larger lumps had to be shattered with the help of a sledge hammer. Later in the week I worked with a fellow about my own age. We were "mucking out", ie. clearing the debris from a rock face following a blasting. This job was partly mechanised – a rocker shovel which could be manoeuvred back and forth on rails and ran on compressed air was driven to scoop up the shattered rock and toss it overhead into a truck behind. Ralph operated the shovel while I made sure the rock reached the truck and pushed it away when full. I had a go on the rocker shovel, unofficially, and soon realised that it was not as easy as it looked. There was real danger in operating such a heavy but mobile piece of equipment in a confined space.

Most of my spare time was spent in riding around West Cornwall on my motor scooter, reading novels, visiting pubs and going along to a folk music club which was held in the former accounts office of the abandoned Botallack Mine known as The Count House. The standard of performance here was very high and the approach to music had a serious and reverent feeling which was new to me. I remember Barbara Wootton, who had a wondeful voice, Mel and Miles, Bill Clifton and John the Fish. The song I remember best was "Down in the Mine" which I enjoyed joining in with and which I could sing with some feeling.

I spent one week machining at 800 feet. My boss was an Italian who spoke little English. We walked for what seemed miles from the shaft until we reached his drill and box of explosives. A hole in the floor of the tunnel indicated where we would be working. My accomplice climbed down a ladder which was hanging from the side of the hole. I handed down the machine, drill steels and explosives, then he asked me to join him. I descended the ladder and had to swing myself onto a ledge which led to the rockface. Most of the stope here appeared to have been worked out; below the ledge was a black void as far as the beam from the light on my helmet could penetrate. I tossed a couple of pieces of rock and they clattered down for several seconds.

We set about drilling a round of holes in the face – I forget how many, but each one took a two foot steel, then a four foot, then a six foot. The job was eventually complete and sticks of explosive were rammed into each hole and all wired up to a single fuse. My Italian driller rolled a cigarette and struck a match on his heel, Clint Eastwood style. He then nonchalantly lit the fuse. By this time I was about to panic – we were stuck on this ledge with that gaping black void and umpteen sticks of gelignite about to go off a few feet away. I scuttled up the ladder and he passed up the equipment. He eventually emerged into the tunnel, obviously enjoying my acute anxiety. After a few seconds there was one helluva bang – not so much heard as felt - I suppose it must be like an earthquake. The floor and walls reverberated as if the earth were being shaken by some mighty hand.

The following week I was put on the nightshift. I was mucking out at 1300 ft. with an old miner – he was over 70 and had retired but couldn't bear being above ground all day so had come back to work. Officially, there had to be a break of 24 hours between a blasting and the subsequent mucking out in order to allow the poisonous fumes to dissipate. Unofficially, the night shift mucked out a few hours after blasting. I suddenly became very ill and started vomiting. After I had thrown up several times at regular intervals my mate told me to retreat to the shaft. I soon felt much better and rejoined him at the rockface where he was working like a Trojan. After a little shovelling I was sick again and retreated once more. I was unable to get to the surface because the ore is raised at night when electricity is cheap so I just had to wait until the end of the shift. That was the only occasion I did night shift.

My last week was spent on tramming, ie. working on the underground trains with their string of wagons. My job was to couple and uncouple the trains and to ride on the end wagon. One had to beware of banging one's head on overhanging rocks. After several trips I managed to persuade my driver to let me take charge of the loco while he rode the end wagon. I got up speed to the normal pace but soon found I was gaining more speed and unable to make the brakes work. I looked round to see my old driver waving frantically from the end of the train. What could I do? The brakes were completely ineffective and we seemed to be heading downhill along a stretch that I'd assumed was quite level. Suddenly we reached a bend and the train veered sideways. It felt for all the world as though the train would leave its tracks and that I'd end up squashed against the rock face. Then the ground began to level out, or slope uphill, and the train came grinding to a halt. My driver ran up to me wild with anger but managing to restrain himself from physical violence.

I remembered much of this as I walked through the straggling, interconnected villages of Boscaswell (where I lodged), Pendeen and Trewellard. There to the right and overlooking the ocean were the three sets of winding gear marking Geevor Mine. Twenty years ago there was only one. I never pursued mining engineering although I certainly was not put off by the time I spent at Geevor. It was rather the attractions of other courses of study which tempted me away. I enjoyed the company of the Geevor miners and was fascinated by the fact that a good half of their number were not Cornish at all, but Russians, Poles, Italians. Many had come here during the last war and taken a job which the West Cornish, with memories of the mine disaster at nearby Levant in 1919 in which 31 men had died, were unwilling to do. These eastern and southern European emigrés usually learned little English but, like the Cornish, lived in old stone cottages and grew vegetables in their gardens and seemed very content with their lot.

I enquired at the garage in Boscaswell whether my landlady was still alive and was amazed to learn that she was, but they could not place the young Ralph who, I remember, had his sights set on Australia and a mining career there, once he had learned his trade at Geevor.

Pendeen had changed little although there seemed to be more attracions for the tourist – restaurants, tea shops and a mining museum at Geevor. As I had missed the pubs, I stopped and treated myself to a Cornish Cream Tea before leaving the village and pressing on. St Just is a rather grim and workaday little town but could never be regarded as just that. Its superb setting amongst tiny, stone-hedged fields and rock-strewn hills, with the granite cliffs and embracing ocean would lend even the most nondescript townscape a certain magic. But St Just does have attractions of its own - the massive, gaunt, non-conformist chapels, the close terraced streets and the occasional palm tree sprouting from a back yard. Leslie Thomas evokes the charm of St Just most eloquently in his book *The Hidden Places of England*. Like the rest of Penwith, St Just reveals a curious mixture of dereliction and development. Whilst there are outcrops of new houses on the edges of some of the villages, there are many deserted old cottages and farmhouses and barns – the sort of places which would be snapped up and converted into retirement and holiday homes further east.

From St Just I headed down the sheltered and lush Cot

Valley to a point a mile or two south of Cape Cornwall. From here I would follow the coast path to Land's End. On the headland was a sign warning of mine shafts. Coming over the top I could see across Whitesand Bay to my journey's end. It was brilliantly sunny and clear – I could not have walked my final few miles under better conditions – I felt moved at the sight of my destination. It was Spring Bank Holiday Sunday and I was to see more walkers in these last couple of hours than I'd seen during the whole three weeks. The rocks are spectacular and Whitesand Bay magnificent.

Trekking across the soft sand below the dunes of Whitesand Bay I considered the possibility of taking a celebratory dip in the ocean. I discarded my shoes and socks and went to paddle. The water felt intensely cold. There was one person swimming, or rather running through the surf trying to pluck up courage to dive in properly. I asked him how he found it. He replied with a strong German accent that it was "so cold". I retreated to my rucksack and redressed my feet. In Sennen I walked past the former coastguard's cottage where my family and I had spent an idyllic week's holiday several years previously. That was during the last week in October - the weather had been mild and sunny and we had enjoyed swimming in Whitesand Bay where the sea had been well warmed after the long hot summer.

I climbed up onto the headland beyond Sennen Cove to walk the final mile to Land's End where the cliffs do not possess a final spectacular dominance but rather peter out in a series of rugged steps down to the swelling sea. I asked a passing tourist, and there were hundreds clambering on the rocks here, to take a photograph of myself as conquering hero. I told him I'd just walked from London – I don't think he believed me. In the absence of a welcoming party I stared back towards Cape Cornwall and west past the Longships and Bishop Rock lighthouses towards the horizon and the unmistakable outline of the Scilly Isles. I bent down to kiss the Land's End granite in true papal fashion, a dramatic moment which served to mark the termination of my three week long-distance walk.

Eventually I struck east and passed a First and Last everything, including a First and Last Craft Workshop(!), the Mead and Scrumpy Exhibition and various other excesses, until I reached the worst excess of all: the official entrance gates where they actually charge you to get to Land's End – well, on second thoughts, perhaps motorists should be charged! At the bus stop I found I'd missed the last bus – it had left at 6.00pm. I intended to stay with friends in Penzance (I had not seen them for four years but had telephoned them a few days previously) and set off along the A30 in that direction. After two or three miles, just below Carn Brea, I telephoned them again. It was of course Bank Holiday Monday and they were out. I guessed they were staying with some mutual friends who live at Sancreed: sure enough I contacted them there. To see two families, very old friends - and all their attendant offspring – after a four year absence, proved a completely agreeable way to end my little adventure.

The next day I caught a train from Penzance which wound its leisurely way back to Westbury in Wiltshire. En route I was able to recognise many a landmark I'd passed on my walk. At Westbury Hazel was waiting and I drove for the first time in three weeks – West Wiltshire flashed past almost unnoticed – such an inferior mode of transport! During the following three weeks my feet grew a new layer of skin and I parted company with four toenails.

Itinerary of route from London to Land's End

Day 1	Chiswick – Addlestone	24 miles
Day 2	Addlestone – High Wycombe	14 miles walked; more by train and bus
Day 3	Marlow – Earley	19 miles
Day 4	Earley – Goring	12 miles
Day 5	Goring – Uffington	23 miles
Day 6	Uffington – Winterbourne Monkton	21 miles
Day 7	Avebury – Netton	27 miles
Day 8	Netton – Ludwell	20 miles walked; 2 hitch-hiked
Day 9	Ludwell – Cerne Abbas	25 miles
Day 10	Cerne Abbas – Bridport	18 miles
Day 11	Bridport – Beer	18 miles
Day 12	Beer – Exeter	18 miles walked; more by bus
Day 13	Exeter – Chagford	20 miles
Day 14	Chagford – Tavistock	7 miles walked; rest hitch-hiked
Day 15	Tavistock – St Neot	23 miles
Day 16	St Neot – Treyarnon Bay	25 miles
Day 17	Treyarnon Bay – Perranporth	21 miles
Day 18	Perranporth – Hayle	20 miles
Day 19	Hayle – Land's End	22 miles
	TOTAL:	377 miles or thereabouts

More books from Ex Libris Press are described on the following pages:

The WALKER'S COMPANION

Edited and Introduced by Roger Jones

Illustrated by Edward Dowden

The works of some 23 writers, beginning with Wordsworth and ending with Henry Willaimson are quoted here and all illustrate some aspect of the walker's art. The urge to get away from it all and get close to nature opens us to the varied pleasures of walking: the pursuit of health, relaxation and renewal. All these are celebrated in prose and poetry. So too are the delights of the country footpath and mountain track, whether they be the fruits of a day's ramble or of an extended walking tour.

The West of England figures prominently in this anthology, in particular Wilkie Collins hiking through Cornwall and excerpts from two accounts of marathon walks undertaken in the last century: Walter White from London to Land's End in 1854 and the American Elihu Burritt walking between the same two points ten years later. The former trekked 425 miles during the month of August on a budget of £10. Both accounts are full of interest and some of the most entertaining and illuminating incidents are quoted in this absorbing collection.

'*This remarkable collection of prose and verse .... a charming ramble of a book*' *Wiltshire Gazette and Herald*

112 pages; full colour cover; 17 pen and ink drawings

ISBN 0 9506563 5 6 Price £2.95

TALL SHIPS IN TORBAY

John Pike

In this book are the stirring events of history: the defeat of the Spanish Armada, the capture of Napoleon and the landing of William, Prince of Orange. Here too are the less familiar episodes: ruthless pirates and their struggles against the Revenue men, the press gangs which terrorised the male population, the provision of support services for the British Fleet anchored in the Bay, local shipbuilding, emigration to the Colonies, the development of the Coastguard Service and the modern fishing industry, and much more.

Tall Ships in Torbay is expertly researched and well documented; it is also fully illustrated with an outstanding collection of pictures and will prove of lasting worth to anyone who knows Torbay or who has a fascination with things maritime.

144 pages; full colour cover; numerous illustrations and map
ISBN 0 948578 03 3 Price £4.95

The above books may be obtained from your local bookshop or from the publisher, post-free, at 1 The Shambles, Bradford on Avon, Wiltshire.

A current list of titles will be sent upon request.

WEST COUNTRY TOUR

John Skinner

Edited and Introduced by Roger Jones

John Skinner is known to some as the author of diaries recording his life and thought as Rector of Camerton in the Somerset Coalfield and as an energetic amateur archaeologist.

Skinner undertook a tour of the West of England in 1797, at the age of 25 and before he found his role in life. In this previously unpublished manuscript we find a young man with a great curiosity to understand and record all he sees during his two months in Somerset, Devon and Cornwall. The resulting diary throws much light on the time when it was written.

Here is social history, topography and autobiography all rolled into one delightful mix.

> '*What makes John Skinner's diary of an excursion through Somerset, Devon and Cornwall in 1797 so notable, is its direct and uncluttered style: it will be of interest to layman and historian alike.*'
>
> James Mildren, *Western Morning News*